The World According to Joan

Also by Joan Collins

Memoirs:
Past Imperfect: An Autobiography (1978)
Katy: A Fight for Life (1982)
Second Act: An Autobiography (1996)

Non-fiction:
The Joan Collins Beauty Book (1980)
Portraits of a Star (1987)
My Secrets (1994)
Health, Youth and Happiness: My Secrets (1995)
My Friends' Secrets (1999)
Joan's Way: Looking Good, Feeling Great (2002)
The Art of Living Well: Looking Good, Feeling Great (2007)

Fiction:
Prime Time (1988)
Love and Desire and Hate (1990)
Too Damn Famous (1995)
Infamous (1996)
Star Quality (2002)
Misfortune's Daughters (2004)

The World According to Joan

Joan Collins

Constable • London

Constable & Robinson Ltd
55–56 Russell Square
London WC1B 4HP
www.constablerobinson.com

First published in the UK by Constable,
an imprint of Constable & Robinson Ltd., 2011

A copy of the British Library Cataloguing in
Publication data is available from the British Library

ISBN 978-1-84901-718-3

Printed and bound in the EU

1 3 5 7 9 10 8 6 4 2

MIX
Paper from
responsible sources
FSC
www.fsc.org
FSC® C018575

For Percy, for always

Contents

Prologue

I love expressing my opinions and ideas on paper, and for several years they have been published by the *Spectator*, *The Times*, the *Daily Mail*, *Harpers Bazaar* and many others. So when Constable & Robinson asked if I would consider gathering all those thoughts and opinions in a book, I was excited and said yes, immediately! Me? Giving my opinions no holds barred? Pen, be the tongue of my mind!

Of course, I've had some practice, having already published two autobiographies, four beauty books, five novels and an inspirational book, but this one would be different.

'I am what I am,' so goes the song written by Jerry

Herman and performed in the musical *La Cage aux Folles* by a female impersonator in drag. And what I am is an illusion. I've often been accused of over-egging the pudding in the costume and make-up department but that's one of the illusions that form a part of what this person called Joan Collins is all about.

That is probably the illusion that the general public sees and remembers the most because spectacular dresses and sharp shoulder-padded suits from *Dynasty* have put that illusion firmly in their minds for ever.

My reality, as I write these words – bare-faced, in jeans and a T-shirt – is quite mundane but I think it's a reality that the public doesn't choose to see. As the showbiz adage goes: that's not what they paid for.

I think they like the glamour girl called Joan Collins, even if they understand glamour is an illusion.

There is already an overabundance of reality in today's world; no secrets for those in the public eye, no hiding place for wrong doers. Everything and everyone is now laid bare for the public to dissect, gossip about and criticize, but now they do it more openly – over the Internet and in the press – just as they used to do over the garden fence in days of yore.

In spite of what you may think or may have read about me, I am actually quite a private person and luckily in the past twenty years since *Dynasty* finished, I have been able to live my life away from the glare of publicity for long stretches. A luxury that most people in my line of business can ill afford.

I don't have a full-time press representative so what comes out in the media aside from work related stuff is what is actually going on in my life: receiving an OBE from the Queen, enduring a dreadful court battle with Random House, going out and about with my friends and family and being happily married for the fifth (and definitely the last!) time to Percy Gibson.

I've always been extremely frank, perhaps too much so. Often friends say to me sarcastically, 'Oh why don't you say what you mean, Joanie!' Well I'm afraid I usually do which is why I have been called opinionated, stubborn, obdurate, headstrong, prejudiced and politically incorrect. Perhaps I am, but I have now reached an age and a stage when I basically do what I like as much as I can, without trying to hurt anyone. For example, I admire Prince Philip's unashamedly 'get on with it' and sometimes politically incorrect attitude towards life and certain people!

I do not tolerate fools lightly, I can't stand being bored or being around bores and I try to live each day to the utmost with passion. I want every day to be a mini-lifetime, in which I achieve something and enjoy something. I try to step back sometimes and appreciate the smaller things in life that can add up to a wonderful whole. When I wake up and stretch, I feel how my whole body responds and enjoys the flexing and use of all those muscles. Then I smell the coffee – it's a great smell. I laugh at a cartoon in my daily paper or relish that first bite of toast and jam.

I make time for fun, and it's not all wining, dining and jetsetting: a game of poker or Scrabble, a night out at the movies or dinner with friends. But I instigate it and am not one of those who waits to be asked. Thomas Jefferson said: 'I find that the harder I work, the more luck I seem to have' and George Bernard Shaw added, 'The only way to avoid being miserable is not to have enough leisure to wonder whether you are happy or not.' These are maxims I live by.

I don't agonize over past failures. What's done is done. I don't cry over spilt milk. As Scarlett O'Hara said, 'I'll think about that tomorrow'. Tomorrow is another day. Onward. I keep on trying to reach my goals and potential. I make plans, even if they might be a touch unrealistic, and I don't give up – ever. To believe in a beautiful future is one of the keys to being happy. As the Desiderata states, 'You are a child of the universe; no less than the trees and the stars, you have a right to be here. With all its sham, drudgery and broken dreams, it is still a beautiful world. Strive to be happy.'

I want to make the most of every day. As our bard proclaimed, life isn't a rehearsal and it races by far too fast not to appreciate it. There'll be plenty of time to sleep when you're dead.

I'm a woman who goes out and gets on with things. I am a doer and I don't sit around wondering what might have been. Crucially, I like myself, and if you don't like yourself not many people will. I don't self-recriminate or over-analyze and *je ne regrette rien*, as Edith Piaf sang.

I am an actress, a writer, a fashion designer. I have produced movies and designed interiors, clothes and jewellery. I've launched my own line of jeans, hats, eye wear, lingerie, blouses and sportswear. I've been the face of a beauty line when most people would tell you it was time to hide it. I adorned posters all over Manhattan for Alexis Bittar jewellery and walked the catwalk for the Red Dress Ball Charity last year. I've had my own perfume and my face has been plastered over 700 magazine covers from the age of seventeen to just a few months ago.

I am a wife, a mother, a grandmother. I have three children whom I love and three grandchildren whom I adore. I am a matriarch and a homemaker. I am a philanthropist and passionate about children. In fact, I'm a philanthropist *with* my children. I am an honorary founding member of the National Society for the Prevention of Cruelty to Children. I have continued to support several foster children in India for over thirty years. In 1988 the Children's Hospital of Michigan honoured me with the Joan Collins Wing and recognition for 'changing the way brain injuries are treated'. I am a patron of the Shooting Star Hospice, which opened its doors to terminally ill children and their families, thanks in part to my fundraising efforts.

I have been divorced four times and happily married to Percy Gibson for nearly ten years. I love travelling but cannot travel light. I love the movies but loathe reality TV, and I love parties when I know most of the people but I hate crowded press events. I adore good food but

I'm not madly keen on cooking. I love designing clothes but wouldn't have a clue how to make them. I love a pristine house but can't use the hoover or washing machine.

I have an abundance of energy (my mother used to call me 'Miss Perpetual Motion' and everyone in our household rues the day they wake up later than I do) but I need eight hours' sleep, and I love a power nap in the afternoon.

I am so positive that my glass is always half full, not half empty, and, like the old joke goes, I believe that there must be a pony in a room full of horse manure. To me, there are two kinds of people in the world: fridges and stoves. People who suck the life out of you are like fridges, making the world cold and dead, and people who enrich you are like stoves, giving off warmth and comfort. I think I am a stove but I know enough to realize that if you don't like me or don't agree with my opinions, well then, maybe this book will leave you cold.* But if you do read it I hope it will inspire and that you don't burn yourself. Perhaps we should have issued a European 'Health and Safety' warning with it.

and since I'm on Twitter, you can send me your own opinions to @joancollinsobe takes to be a star – as if they knew the real meaning of the word.

What they crave is fame and adulation, which they think will cure their ills and make them live happily ever after – how naive!

I think that too much of today's TV is coarse, repellent, amateurish and puerile. It has lost its true entertainment value and seems driven by reality shows that feed off people so thrilled to be on TV and becoming famous that they will humiliate themselves for the price of a train ticket.

Having occasionally watched the deluded souls on *Big Brother* and similar reality shows, my heart goes out to these poor creatures/contestants. Their belief as they flaunt their meagre talents that the all-encompassing pill called fame is going to change their sad lives is pathetic. As they bleat on about wanting to be famous or 'living the dream', they don't understand the pitfalls and sacrifices of such a hollow aim.

There have been so many dead celebrities who became so trapped and persecuted by their hard-earned fame that they were unable to cope with real life: Elvis Presley, Marilyn Monroe and Michael Jackson spring instantly to mind, but there are dozens, probably hundreds of others who, in their quest for this elusive will o' the wisp have fallen by the wayside. River Phoenix overdosed on drugs; John Belushi became a victim of drugs and obesity; and more recently the extremely talented Heath Ledger overdosed on prescription medications. He was awarded a posthumous Oscar for his chilling performance in *The Dark Knight* but what good did it do him – he simply couldn't cope with life in the fishbowl called fame.

And of course poor Marilyn Monroe, a simple woman sick to death of the studio system that had ruled her life. I met her when I first went to Hollywood under contract to Fox. She told me how the studio bosses treated the startlets like whores and if they didn't comply with the contract they would be dropped. She was sweet, vulnerable and sad and her unmade-up face and messy hair were a far cry from the image that Fox wanted her to promote.

Fame has an even darker, more complicated side. Many celebrities rely on hangers on and false friends who try to take advantage of them. Then there are the stalkers who consume or kill those they are obsessed with. I used this theme in my novel *Too Damn Famous*. The main character is a fictional, famous soap-star icon who searches for true love but only finds men who want to use her for her status. This is sadly true for many famous actresses: look at the brilliant Sandra Bullock, who after receiving the accolade of her life – the Oscar – tragically discovers that her husband, the aptly named Jesse James, has cheated on her with a tattooed stripper.

Jill Dando, the pretty British presenter and TV commentator was murdered on her doorstep by a crazed stalker. Jill wasn't looking for fame, it was a by-product of her job. John Lennon's musical gifts propelled him to stardom but his killer was so deluded that he thought he could morph into Lennon if he killed him.

Most extremely famous television and movie stars need a huge amount of protection from certain members of the public, particularly because of the recent emergence of the dedicated Facebook warriors and fanatics who devour every word about their idols in the plethora of Internet sites, gossip magazines and TV shows. Some celebrities are tracked online 24/7 by services that employ paparazzi to keep tabs on them, wherever they may be. Elizabeth Hurley told me that during her break-up with Hugh Grant, in order to escape the paparazzi camped outside her home she had to leave the house 'before 7 a.m. and return after 11 p.m.' The week before my wedding to Percy, a regular rota of paps camped outside my flat day and night and we were photographed anytime we came in and out. At one point Percy went out shopping with a driver who engaged in a high speed chase with a paparazzo (whose Vauxhall Vectra was no match for the BMW 7 series Percy was in). Percy told me he'd never been quite so ill in his life after that. And coming out of Percy's stag party (which I'd crashed) we opened the door to face a firing squad of what felt like fifty photographers snapping their flashers: 'I can't see,' said Percy, to which I retorted 'And I can't stand!'

When I was in the middle of a messy divorce from Peter Holm (Husband No. 4), I went into my garden in LA one morning and whilst I was deadheading some hydrangeas, I heard a strange screaming from a helicopter overhead. It was a paparazzo famous for stalking people who was hanging out of the craft by his legs, furiously snapping away at me. Talk about invasion of privacy! I yelled and waved at him to go away but this just gave him a better picture.

But why do some people become famous whilst others, even if extremely talented and attractive, never manage to do so? I was extremely fortunate at being discovered at seventeen while still a student at RADA. I was doing some photographic modelling for magazines to supplement my paltry pocket money when, lo and behold, an agent saw my pictures and whisked me off to the film studios to be tested, just like it happens in the movies.

I realized I was one lucky young girl, but then I had paid my dues in acting classes, repertory companies and touring the UK in several plays. When I was nine and attending a theatrical school, to my great delight I was chosen to play one of the young sons in Ibsen's *A Doll's House* at the Arts Theatre in London. My 'brother' Judith and I were thrilled to bits on the opening night – cute as buttons in our little nineteenth-century sailor suits. But as the days turned into weeks, we got bored waiting for our two very short scenes and sat backstage playing games and reading comic books. One night we were so engrossed in snakes and ladders that we completely missed our entrance. The director stormed in yelling bloody murder, pushed us to the front of the stage, where we managed to stammer out our few lines in floods of tears. After the curtain came down the director screamed at us in front of the entire cast: 'You've neither the talent nor the intelligence to become actresses, and you never will!' I was mortified and learned then and there that acting was, like flying, 'hours of tedium followed by a few minutes of sheer panic.' You have to have the stamina to endure constant boredom and rejection but the payoff of your moment in the sun is sheer bliss and makes it all worth it.

After my first term at RADA, my father, in a complete turnabout from his theatricals-are-vulgar-common-and-coarse philosophy and constant entreaties to 'go to secretarial school and find a good husband', decided to back me in my acting career and invest in a repertory company in Maidstone. I was assistant-assistant stage manager, assistant-assistant prop-master and I under-studied the maid in *Private Lives*, the maid in *French without Tears*, and the maid in *Dangerous Corner*.

One night I had to bring the curtain down at the end of the show. I managed to pull the heavy curtain down with all my strength. I was, however, unable to bring it back up for the bows. The actors stood furiously in behind the curtain, attempting to swat it open so they could take their bows. The applause gradually died and was replaced by giggles and guffaws of the audience seeing the curtain moving frenetically like something possessed. I tugged away madly but it wouldn't budge. Finally my terrified red face popped out from the side of the stage in plain sight of the audience, as I called frantically to the stage manager on the other side. I chose my words poorly: 'I can't get it up!' Hysterical laughter erupted.

The next day, while I was walking around town, I

overhead a shopkeeper sniggering about the previous night's disaster. 'It was all that young girl's fault. Some rich man's daugh-er, born with a silver spoon in her mouf and can't do a bleeding thing – wha' a farce, eh?' It was then and there that I made up my mind: I would make my own way, and get my own jobs without any help from anyone, particularly Daddy.

When I began to study to become an actress, I didn't think about wanting fame. I just wanted to act because I loved it. And I learned early on that I needed to be the best I could be at my job after the initial infatuation with my youth, beauty and sex appeal had eventually worn out. I knew I'd need some additional skill sets in case work inevitably dried up so I began studying interior design and started writing.

When I first went to California and furnished my Los Angeles apartment I bought a television and fridge from none other than the famous 1940s actor Victor Mature. He had wisely turned his fame and the money he'd made into a chain of electrical-appliance stores. 'The sweet life don't last for ever, honey,' he informed me, grinning Samson-like from behind the counter, 'so put some away while you can.'

During *Dynasty* the young actor John James, who played Jeff Colby, was always on the phone. This often irritated John Forsythe, who played the irascible Blake Carrington. 'What's that boy doing?' he grumbled. 'Always on the phone – he's not going to have much of a career if he's never on set on time.' As it turned out our JJ was talking to his broker every day and following the stock market avidly. He ended up with the last laugh when *Dynasty* finished as he was rich and had invested in property, made a fortune in the financial world and made enough excellent investments to say 'I don't have to worry about getting an acting job any more – ever!' Clever boy.

Up until only a decade or two ago, fame lacked the kudos that it seems to have now. It used to be thought that the entertainment business, whilst offering escapism, was no substitute for the true accomplishments and fortunes of real life – better health, a higher standard of living and a balanced and just society. People certainly didn't seem to crave fame like they do today. My father, who was a theatrical agent, often told me: 'Most theatricals are vulgar, common and coarse, and if that's the profession you want to be in, then you'll become just like them.' Well, hopefully I didn't become any of those things, maybe partly due to his advice, which helped me keep a balanced head on my shoulders. Unfortunately, not all celebrities had a father as wise as mine. He told me never to rely on anyone else for money: 'You have to do everything for yourself and by yourself,' he would say. And his advice paid off. My sister Jackie and brother Bill have both made their own way in life, and their own money.

By the time *Dynasty* came my way I had been an actress for nearly thirty years so I was fully prepared for fame. Or so I thought until I found myself under a barrage of adulation and fan mania. It was insane, and I do not miss that part one bit, although, without wishing to blow my own trumpet, I do admit that the adoration and praise heaped upon all of the *Dynasty* cast was not surprising: the show was a number one hit around the world for years, and received dozens of awards. John Forsythe, Linda Evans and I also became the recipients of many more but, as the great wit Billy Wilder said, 'Awards are like piles: eventually every asshole gets one!'

The attention was so great that sometimes I couldn't walk down the street without being followed by paparazzi and I was asked for autographs constantly, even when I was with my daughter and browsing the lingerie rails. (Paul Newman told me that he'd stopped signing autographs after a fan followed him into the men's room and slipped a piece of paper under the door of his stall asking for his signature.) Often I chose to stay at home rather than face a world seething with 'paps' or whatever other surprises my celebrity might spring upon me.

During the late eighties some fans were so over-enthusiastic that it was impossible to go into boutiques without being approached. So, one day I came up with what I thought would be a crafty solution to avoid attention. In London I found a shop that sold all-encompassing black burkas. I bought one, and the following day put it on. I then walked clumsily down the front steps of my building for a bit of hopefully anonymous retail therapy. With only a slit for my eyes, I felt like a walking tomb. Without peripheral vision I immediately tripped over the flapping hem and hit the ground. As billowing folds of black fabric became caught between my legs, I tumbled unceremoniously down to the pavement to the puzzlement of my neighbours.

Reclaiming my dignity, I awkwardly righted myself, pulled my burka around me and attempted to cross the road at Belgrave Square, where the cars all seemed to be driven by aspiring Jackie Stewarts. Since I was unable to see either to the right or left out of the eye slits, I stumbled across the street, tripping again over my voluminous garb. Drivers cursed and I was unable to get a taxi to stop for me (they acted as if I were invisible, which, of course, was partly my aim). I managed to stumble to nearby Miss Selfridge where, finally, covered in sweat and totally exhausted, I went into a changing room and ripped the damn thing off. The burka went to a charity shop and I felt sorry for the poor women forced to constantly wear this ungainly garment. However, I must admit *nobody* recognized me.

Why is fame used as the goal of existence for so many people? Innumerable shows are created to capitalize on this phenomenon. These fame-makers of today reflect a negative cycle, where media fuels the desires of society to seek only fame and society demands from the media more and more examples where fame and fortune can be attained without any effort. Producers of reality shows feed the fame frenzy by filming so-called ordinary people and turning them into famous people. So some viewers feel 'If they can do it – so can I'. As the shows celebrate bad behaviour and stupidity, each show seems to become more and more idiotic. But this is not the duty of entertainment and art: their duty is to elevate and challenge, not to glorify degradation, rudeness and abuse. I also believe the arts have an even more important task: to hold a mirror up to life and reveal our weaknesses by mocking them and our strengths by inspiring them. There's very little to feel inspired by when watching reality programmes.

Yale University recently issued results of a poll showing the aspirations of young graduates: to be a CEO of a major company; to be a senator; to be a doctor or to be the personal assistant (a 'gofer') to a celebrity. Forty-two per cent of the respondents chose to be a gofer. We are so celebrity-obsessed that even the sharpest minds become dulled by it. Another recent poll of 3,000 children aged five to eleven found that only 6 per cent wanted to be doctors and only 4 per cent wanted to be teachers. More than a third wanted to be pop stars, models, movie stars or sports stars. Two thirds of teachers questioned said their students craved fame but had only a vague idea of the talent required.

We have instant coffee, instant food, instant communication and now we want 'insta-celebs' – either to become one or to watch one – without any irony or reflective (self)mockery.

It reminds me of the story of the organ-grinder's monkey who was asked by a bird sitting on a pole, 'Why would you do that, wouldn't you rather be swinging freely from trees and roaming your native land?' The monkey replied: 'What? And give up show business?'

Fame brings about delusions of grandeur as well – very much like a drug. Arnold Schwarzenegger and Tiger Woods are a case in point. No man in his right mind would believe he could have affairs with more than a dozen women without it being revealed. But the millions upon millions of dollars foisted upon famous individuals nowadays can easily make them feel as if they are untouchable. The illusion of power is one of the greatest aphrodisiacs; likewise, the outing of this kind of delusion is one of the greatest levellers. Just look at crooks like Bernard Madoff. Similarly, Ryan Giggs, the premiership footballer, had an affair with his sister-in-law, and then wanted her to have an abortion. The list is endless, just read any tabloid each Sunday.

Charlie Sheen is another one whose head has been turned by the delusion of fame. 'I'm on a drug and it's called Charlie Sheen,' he brags. 'No one else can handle it.' He has two porn stars looking after his infant twins and lets TV cameras film him urinating and giving blood to prove he is not on drugs – how utterly pathetic. However, he got his comeuppance when his one-man show at Radio City Music Hall was less than half full and people booed all the way through.

On *X-Factor*, people of little or no talent are assembled on a weekly basis to be praised to the skies or jeered by a ravenous crowd, not unlike gladiators at the Roman Circus. 'The *X-Factor* gives everyone the chance to be a star,' the voiceover says. Maybe. But more than that, what it actually does give is the chance for everyone to be humiliated. When Simon Cowell told one boy band that they were the worst group he'd ever heard, the poor schmucks actually grinned as if he'd paid them a compliment, so thrilled were they to have their fifteen minutes – or in their case two minutes – of fame. One singer, who performed 'My Way' with a mere modicum of talent, was greeted with an audience so enthusiastic it was as if he was the second coming of Sinatra himself. As the panel praised him, you could almost see the poor fellow's chest swell with pride, as his eyes lit up with the expectation of the fame elixir.

Pre-eighties fan magazines – *Motion Picture*, *Photoplay* and *Modern Screen* – featured glamour layouts and saccharine-sweet at-home pictures of stars and their families masterminded by the studio publicist, all tastefully stage managed. The star was never allowed to look anything but perfect and woe betide them if they failed to live up to this ideal. When I was under studio contract I was often chastised for my bohemian way of dressing and sometimes received a slap on the hand from my studio. (How ironic that as one hand slapped 'naughty Joanie', the other was trying to get into her Capris. Double standards were rife, and the studio head who told me he could make me 'the most famous star on the lot if [I] would be *nice*' to him was also a happily married man.) Many actresses and actors were under the watch of a mentor, often an important producer or head of studio who looked after the performer and made sure their career was thriving.

One night at a party at Gene Kelly's house I sidled up to the bar and sat next to a rather nondescript blonde sitting alone. Suddenly she turned to me and said, 'Fox wanted me to play the *Girl in the Red Velvet Swing*, but then they said I'm too old.' That's when the penny dropped – this was the fabled Marilyn Monroe.

As we sat and drank martinis we became quite pally and she whispered, 'Watch out for the wolves in Hollywood, honey.'

'Oh, I can handle wolves.'

'Not the power bosses. The casting couch rules here. They just love to push us girls around. 'Specially watch out for Zanuck,' – the head of the studio – 'if he doesn't get what he wants, honey, he'll drop your contract. It's happened to lots of girls.'

'Well, thanks for the advice, I'll definitely keep away from him.'

Prophetically, at the studio a few days later Zanuck pounced on me. Breathing cigar fumes, he hissed, 'You haven't had anyone till you've had me, honey. I'm the biggest and the best and I can go all night.' I was so shocked I couldn't think of anything to say so I wriggled free and ran back to the set, and the fact that I didn't retort or snitch probably saved my contract, because I heard that a starlet who had been dropped had riposted to his 'Baby, I'm the biggest in the business' by squealing, 'You better be, honey, 'cause you're only five foot two!'

The studio did everything in its power to protect their precious stars from scandal. No hint of bad behaviour, be it drunkenness, adultery, drug taking or – heaven forbid – homosexuality, ever made the papers. If the public had known that JFK was an inveterate womanizer, that Marilyn Monroe was an insecure pill-popper who was always late for work; that Rock Hudson was gay and that Joan Crawford was a drunken harridan who abused her kids, they would never have become the admired people that they did. The publicists of the day saw to that. They kept the media at their command because Hollywood was in the business of selling beautiful lifestyles and beautiful dreams that people could aspire to. They did not want to show the warts-and-all harsh realities that we read avidly about today. Where has the mystique gone?

Now, not only are the warts revealed, but also every possible flaw. Actors and actresses, from A-list to Z-list have their clothes and physical appearance discussed, lampooned and scrutinized. Even wonky toes or a bad case of acne are criticized! The public adores pictures of bedraggled celebs falling drunkenly out of nightclubs, of actresses baring their cellulite on the beach, actors patting their wobbly beer bellies or balding pates and pregnant starlets proudly showing us their naked baby bump. Is nothing sacred any more? What's next? A pair of wanna-be slebs showing us their bedroom manoeuvres? Many people want to look down at stars in the gutter rather than put them on a pedestal.

In the past, image was everything; today it seems to

exist only on the red carpet. Real stars reach the top of the heap by their talent and a little bit of luck, not on their backs. But from the indiscretions and peccadilloes we read about today, you wouldn't think so. Very little shocks the people any more. They are avid to know more details – Lindsay in rehab and jailed again? That's great – more tabloid magazines will be sold. Britney Spears shaving her head? Why not? She started a trend.

Today's celebrities are a world away from those of Hollywood's Golden Age. There are no illusions about anyone any more. We know how Sarah Jessica Parker looks without make-up as she takes out the rubbish. We have seen a thousand blurry snaps of celebrities drunk or snorting cocaine – there is no more magic. (And there is no privacy either. When I had a slight Victorian swoon at the *Vanity Fair* party I was whisked away discreetly in an ambulance via the back door rather than have to face a phalanx of photographers at the entrance, but then someone called the press and it was all over the media the following day.)

Why do today's famous women all look vaguely similar? Do they think the cookie-cutter look is a key to success? From their hair, make-up and clothes to those ludicrous shoes they all wear (which, incidentally and according to Dr Rock Positano, the New York foot expert, will ruin their feet within a few years). In the past, one would never mistake film star Veronica Lake for Ava Gardner, Claudette Colbert for Lana Turner or Lauren Bacall for Marilyn Monroe. They were total individuals with raw talent, who worked hard and developed their own distinctive 'look'. They did *not* want to look like any other star. Today though, many of the under-thirties are indistinguishable from each other. All the actresses on the many TV cop shows appear to be wearing the same grey or black suit and white shirt. On the red carpet they're all in strapless gowns with minimal jewellery and simple hair and make-up. I mourn the passing of Elizabeth Taylor for many reasons, glamour least among them but now that she has died there are only a few great screen icons still with us – Sophia Loren, Lauren Bacall and Barbra Streisand, long may they live.

I met Elizabeth Taylor on my first visit to LA. She had just married her third husband, film-producer Michael Todd. Not only was she a true beauty, she was down-to-earth and fun, with a wonderful wicked giggle. Having been a star since age seven she knew how to behave like one.

We dined in a restaurant on the Sunset Strip called La Rue. We were both dressed to the nines in satin, cocktail dresses, mink but of course she was wearing a ton of diamonds and jewels. I'd admired Elizabeth since I'd first seen her on screen in *Lassie*. She deserved the accolades for her beauty, sheer star power and the epic quality of her lifestyle. The last time I saw her was when we were working together on the movie *These Old Broads*. She was still beautiful and larger than life in personality and *joie de vivre* but had difficulty walking. On the first day of shooting we had to do a publicity shoot on the set. Four director's chairs were artfully arranged on a small dais and Elizabeth, Shirley MacLaine, Debbie Reynolds and I were seated in them in full glamorous gear. But the photographer was in a complete state of nerves. Flustered and red faced, he kept rearranging the chairs until Liz told him to 'Get on with it, dear.'

'Oh yes, ma'am,' stuttered the snapper, 'I mean – Lady Elizabeth – sorry, sorry, Dame – yes, Dame Taylor – oh hell, what do I call you?'

'Dame Elizabeth,' cackled La Liz. 'You can all call me *Dame* Elizabeth.'

'Even on the call sheet!?' asked an anxious assistant director.

'Oh yes,' giggled Elizabeth, winking at all of us on the dais. 'On the call sheet and on my chair, *everyone* must call me Dame Elizabeth.'

'I've earned it!' she whispered as Debbie and Shirley fell about laughing. 'But you gals can just call me Elizabeth' – she hated to be called Liz.

A few years after she had retired, I met the dangerously gorgeous superstar Ava Gardner, who often modestly claimed she couldn't act. She still had that indispensable star power that can't be manufactured, even though she wore plain clothes and little make-up. It was a magical presence combined with alluring beauty and the ability to make headlines effortlessly. I'll never forget seeing her for the first time at the Embassy Club in London. I suppose her date had been treating her very badly, and she was crying and having a screaming argument with him, yet she looked entrancing and powerful, like some sort of jungle cat fiercely protecting her territory. Years later this image came back to me powerfully when I was thinking about how to play Alexis.

Of course, the ultimate celebrity of all time is still Marilyn Monroe. In the nearly fifty years since her death, hundreds of books have been written about her and her classic beauty still looks modern. I wonder how many of today's sub-lebrities will ever achieve that degree of long-term adulation?

During the years of *Dynasty*, I was falsely accused by the media of extraordinarily bad behaviour – everything from stubbing out a cigarette on a fur coat, slipping on a lettuce leaf as I left a restaurant in a huff or having a screaming hissy fit in my dressing room because I didn't like my dialogue in a scene. I was also accused of having relationships with a string of men, many of whom I'd never met! None of this was true but due to my successful portrayal of a devious manipulative bitch the public longed to think that that is who I was. But at least it meant that, when I was recognized, there was a certain amount of respect from the public, and most of the time the paps kept their distance – relatively! I pity poor Robert Pattinson, who can go nowhere without being mobbed by teenage groupies and when in New York has to hide in his hotel room.

The paparazzi stalk their victims today like big game hunters stalk endangered species. As photographers stand in front of the car of some hapless celeb, preventing the poor driver from moving, they bleat 'We're only doing our job'. The media beast has an insatiable appetite which needs to be slaked by more and more outrageous behaviour. However, if one really steps out of line like Mel Gibson, who was recorded abusing his girlfriend and then insulting Jews and Blacks alike with racist rants, the end is nigh. He was fired from a movie, and then said he is quitting show business and moving to Australia. 'I'm done with Hollywood, they can all fuck off. I don't need any of them. I've had it with fame, it's destroying me,' Gibson ranted.

Demi Moore became so sick of fame after she bared her naked bump for famous photographer Annie Liebowitz on the cover of *Vanity Fair* that she upped sticks and moved to Idaho. This was considered high art at the time but a couple of years later every pregnant starlet was posing naked and pregnant and it just looked tacky. When she returned to Hollywood and hooked up with a younger guy, the fame came back with all the attendant snide and crude remarks. Demi fights back by constantly tweeting to answer rumours and innuendo and by posting cute little pictures of her and Ashton Kutcher cuddling under the covers online. With two million twitter followers, she's cleverly harnessing the new media to her advantage and trying to control her fame the way the old-fashioned publicists controlled the fame of their obedient stars back in the Golden Age.

One of the saddest things about the reality stars is that

they combine a complete lack of sense of self-awareness and irony with a huge sense of entitlement. They believe they are owed fame simply because they crave it. 'I want the whole world to know who I am – it would be priceless, like Mastercard,' said one young girl. 'I wanna be somebody – I yearn to be somebody people talk about,' bleated another young man. They beg and plead to stay on programmes like *Big Brother* – but it isn't only for fame, it's also for the money, and particularly the notoriety. Being photographed in the *Sun* or *OK!* would be their highest achievement.

Some reality stars do transcend temporary popularity but they are the rare exception, such as the talented Susan Boyle, Leona Lewis and Will Young. A large percentage of 'the winners' of these shows have rarely been heard from again. Their little bubble of fame burst and left them but their lives will never be the same again.

Two of the biggest cover girl stars in America, featured in all the celebrity magazines, are Kim Kardashian and Kate Gosselin. Neither are actresses or models or have any discernible talent, yet the media fawns upon them as if they were Elizabeth Taylor in her heyday. The week that Elizabeth died, two magazines had her on the cover but the rest displayed Kim Kardashian's toothy grin. As for Gosselin, her claim to fame is a boring reality show featuring her family of eight children and a surly, unattractive husband. For some unknown reason the public loved this ménage and she has continued to go from strength to strength in the fame game with zero attributes of talent or ability or any skills except for marketing herself cleverly enough to stay in the public eye. It's beyond comprehension, yet how many thousands of young people think 'If she can do it, without talent or skill, then so can I'? Instant fame has nothing to do with dedication or even hard work – it's just 'Look at me, I'm outrageous'. Most are devoid of talent, beauty or charm and to stay in the public eye they have had to rely on self-serving antics, each time more bizarre or licentious. From Monica Lewinsky to the WAGS and the hookers who bonk sports stars or flash their knickers at the drop of a flash bulb, to the dozens of girls who came out of the closet in the Tiger Woods scandal, their fame will be fleeting.

Sadly, the television bosses realize it's cheaper to make reality shows with unknowns who might become famous or with wannabes desperate for fifteen minutes of fame than to produce sitcoms or dramas in which they have to pay professional actors and writers.

Within a short time most go from the glitter to the gutter because this type of fame is fleeting.

Real celebrities of the golden age of cinema – the likes of Clark Gable, Bette Davis, Elizabeth Taylor – were great actors with incredible talent which also brought them fame. Today's actors such as George Clooney, Brad Pitt and Angelina Jolie do deserve the exaltation they receive, especially as they swim in a sea of thousands who don't. They have the *real* X factor.

When Tony Curtis died in 2010 the world gave him a prolonged ovation, even though he hadn't had real fame for many decades. But he was a true movie icon, whose fame was nurtured and manufactured by the now defunct Hollywood studio system. He was part of the last wave of contract players signed up in the forties and fifties. Among them were Elizabeth Taylor, Kim Novak, Debbie Reynolds, Rock Hudson, Jayne Mansfield and little ol' me! We contractees were taught how to act and behave by our studios but they completely controlled us. Their gruelling training would make *X-Factor* boot camp seem like a day at Disneyland. How to walk, talk, dance, fence, ride a horse and pose for endless publicity stills was our daily grind. The peccadilloes of contractees would be controlled by the ruthless publicists from the studios, who in their turn controlled the few purveyors of the severely white-washed gossip magazines. The gossip columnists Hedda Hopper and Louella Parsons were so influential they could ruin a young player's burgeoning career if he or she did anything out of line, and so the studios and their PRs worked hand-in-hand with the actors to maintain discipline. They also courted the formidable Hedda and Louella and each Christmas their cars would be filled to the brim with the most expensive gifts from every studio head, star and producer.

Hedda Hopper interviewed me when I first went to Hollywood. At twenty-one I had little to offer in terms of sophisticated or witty repartee and not much idea of how to groom myself either. To meet the scary gorgon legend for tea I wore my usual uniform of jeans and plaid shirt and my hair was long and messy. Miss Hopper did not take to me at all and her column was less than flattering. It ended with 'Joan Collins looks like she combs her head with an egg beater'. Three years later, I was living with a young and unknown (at the time) actor called Warren Beatty and when Hedda heard about this she warned my studio 'that girl would ruin her career' if I continued cohabiting so flagrantly. The studio heeded her words and told us to get married or stop living together. Times sure have changed – nowadays that liaison would have been a great way to jump-start a career and gain lots of stories in the tabloids!

When I won my first major role as the eponymous *Girl in the Red Velvet Swing* the studio launched an extensive publicity campaign to make me known to the public. My job included not just acting but also endless days being photographed, looking 'soulful', 'cute' or 'pinuppy'; dozens of interviews with journalists from all over the USA and Europe; countless stage-managed appearances at premieres of 20th Century Fox movies (often with an escort approved by the studio, who didn't approve of Warren Beatty: 'He's not famous, and he's got pimples' one of Fox's reps told me). Needless to say, I did attend public premieres with only studio-approved companions: Robert Wagner, Jeff Hunter and strangely enough Elizabeth Taylor's ex, Nick Hilton.

The premieres were pretty tame events then, unlike the fan mania that happens at premieres today with barricades, police and screaming fans kept away from the stars. However famous the star, fans and photographers respectfully kept their distance then and there was little familiarity. Famous stars being stalked wherever they went by phalanxes of ravenous paparazzi was totally unheard of and would have been frowned upon by the powerful studios.

Brad Pitt and Angelina Jolie (or Brangelina as they are known) can't take their kids anywhere without paparazzi swarming all over them. Russell Brand's wife, Katy Perry, had a photographer try to stick his camera up her skirt, so Brand bopped him one. Did the pap get the blame? Of course not – Russell Brand faced charges for assault. An obviously upset Catherine Zeta Jones, arriving at the airport to attend her ailing husband Michael Douglas, was confronted by a pack of paparazzi. When she tearfully asked to please be left alone, they refused. There's too much money in that sad-faced picture of her and they don't give a fig about her distress.

Now, to make matters worse, *TMZ*, a nightly pro-gramme in the USA, specializes in videotaping famous people coming out of restaurants, clubs or airports. The photographers ask questions, which they hope the celebrity will answer and the following night the footage is analyzed by a soppy-looking group of twenty-somethings who talk about that star's behaviour and attitude and make fun of them in a nasty sneering way.

I was recently confronted by ten paparazzi as I left a restaurant with a friend. The restaurant was over the road from my home so I walked, and the paps followed me all the way, snapping feverishly and asking mundane and stupid questions like, 'Hey, why do you think you look so good? What's your secret?' and more personal ones such as, 'Where's your husband?' and 'Whatcha doing these days?' Sure enough, the following day *TMZ* showed this footage and the commentators then chatted about me and my looks. 'Hey, where's she been? She looks hot,' and 'What, she's *how* old?' and 'Wow, she sure looks good.' High praise indeed but reading what some people post on Facebook, Twitter and various blogs the insults could have been overwhelming.

But that's the price of fame now. W.C. Fields once said, 'If you can't take the heat get outta the kitchen' and since I still work and enjoy it I'll continue until my kitchen doesn't cook any more!

Today's public wants its celebs younger and younger. Justin Bieber is seventeen and the top performer in the USA; Willow Smith, the actor Will Smith's precocious ten-year-old daughter, is a dress designer and has made several music videos; and one of the recent Oscar nominees was fourteen-year-old Hailee Steinfeld, who sounded as if she were thirty. What next: toddlers in tights and stilettos on *Dancing with the Stars*? Shirley Temple, eat your heart out!

As the song says: 'Fame, if you win it, comes and goes in a minute.' Where's the real stuff in life to cling to? 'Love is the answer, someone to love is the answer.' And that's what I believe in – true love, from your family and good friends, trumps all. Especially fifteen minutes of fame.

seem to minister to their kids' every need. During these holidays, the quiet of my rural idyll in the hills of the South of France is punctuated by the demanding sound of the rugrats' voices raised high above the entreating voices of their parents, who seem to follow them around in supplication.

At the risk of offending everybody under the age of fifteen, and maybe my children, too, I must admit that today's little darlings could learn a lot from generations past.

Everything has changed so radically since I was a kid. At fifteen I was still playing with dolls (which seems hard to believe – even for me – when, less than two years later, I was appearing in my first film, *Lady Godiva Rides Again* in which I had one line as a seventeen-year-old beauty contestant playing alongside such veterans as Diana Dors and Kay Kendall). When I read about the Princesses Elizabeth and Margaret growing up in a more innocent age, I was gratified to learn that they, like other children of their generation, often relied on their imagination to amuse themselves. It was a time when painting, writing, doing jigsaw puzzles and word games and reading were encouraged when children were only allowed a few outings per year – which usually the Christmas pantomime. I must admit I did rather better than that: I was allowed to see one movie a week (and sometimes with special permission I was able to see two per week). I listened to the radio and watched our new TV (that was dull and showed only sports and politics, which I wasn't interested in anyway). What a stark contrast to today's youngsters, who idle away hours in front of their television or hunch over their computers. On early morning television, every channel airs cartoons, interspersed with commercials showing products, encouraging two to twelve years olds to persuade their parents to buy them. And sadly it works.

When I was a girl I was lucky if my parents actually acknowledged my existence, let alone tried to please me. The highlight of the week was a long car trip with the whole family to visit my grandmothers in Brighton or Bognor – and how boring was that!

But like all children – of any generation – I also tried to get my own way. One afternoon I came home from the cinema to be greeted by my father, who announced that we would be going to the pictures as a treat that evening. Not realizing there was a limit on amusements, I happily declared what a fine day this was turning into, as I had already seen one movie earlier that afternoon with my mother. My father curtly informed me I had therefore had my quota of fun, and would not be going to the pictures that evening after all. 'It's bad for your brain,' he announced. 'Too much stimulation.' And I think he was right – there *is* such a thing as too much stimulation: you have only to look at the baffled, vacant stare of children when parents turn off the television or rip electronic gadgets from their tiny paws.

So I obeyed my father when he said I couldn't see another movie and since I would never have dreamed of questioning my parents' authority I took it as given that they had the final word on all things. Yet today's mini-me's seem to take their parents' orders as an opener to a debate. Pleas and supplications turn into manoeuvring and cajoling worthy of a UN summit, until out-and-out crying or faces of utter misery convince their buckling parents to give in to desperate demands for new toys or outings. As I watch my own children and daughter-in-law crumble in the face of this childish opposition, I wonder how so much could have changed in so little time.

Similar to other children of the pre-sixties generation, my treats and sweets were rare and we only had a few toys. Imagine this now! Most children would go on strike if this were their lot. But I had a vivid imagination. I thought of becoming a perfumer and decided to please my mother with some exquisite scent. I collected dozens of rose petals from the park and put them in a jam jar with some rose water. I left the mixture for a fortnight hoping it would now be a delicious scent, but to my horror when I opened it the jar was seething with maggots!

I was lucky to receive one or two presents at Christmas, and it was the same for my birthday, when the entertainment usually consisted of having a couple of school friends over for tea, some cucumber sandwiches, and a slice of cake; if it was very special, a candle might be added. Today, hundreds, sometimes thousands of pounds are spent on children's gifts and parties. I know of one cleaning lady who makes only £12,000 a year but who spent £2,000 on a computer as a birthday present for her daughter. And in star-studded celebrityville, the likes of Tom Cruise hire an entire circus for their little darlings' birthdays. It's out of control. One Christmas Aaron Spelling ordered fake snow to cover the backyard and garden of his palatial mansion when he gave a party for his daughter Tori. Gwen Stefani and Gavin Rossdale allegedly spent a whopping $15,000 orchestrating 'A bouncy castle, three birds, a face painter, a balloon artist, and roaming superhero characters' which entertained 100 party guests, who feasted on 'burgers, hot dogs, tacos, quesadillas, French fries and chicken fingers'. A candy-floss machine and a lemonade stand rounded out the bonanza! Angelina Jolie and Brad Pitt supposedly bought their four-year-old daughter Shiloh a jeep that is safe for kids, and apparently he's thinking of getting her a toy ATV that she can drive around the property.

Britney Spears reportedly threw a double birthday party for her little boys. The car and truck themed bash included customized mini-motorized trucks and featured tattoo-inspired decals and personalized plates. The birthday boys drove around the party in their trucks and feasted on a yellow, truck-shaped cake.

As for Christmas, when I was growing up nobody even thought about it until the second week of December. The shops were not brimming with every imaginable gadget, toy or decoration and the ghastly consumerism that now starts in October did not exist. We would all marvel at the nativity scene at school and ponder on the spirituality of the occasion, or how Mary managed to get pregnant.

Today, Christmas seems to be all about what you can get, instead of what it means to give. Surely the idea of *giving* is the important message we should be instilling in our children?

When I go on holiday with my daughter, Tara, my daughter-in-law, Angela, who is married to my son, Sacha, Tara's two children, Miel, twelve, and Weston, seven, and Sacha and Angela's daughter, Ava Grace, also seven, every time we venture into Saint Tropez or the markets of Ramatuelle, toys are not just a special treat, they are these kids' 'human rights'. If we don't buy them anything we become the worst kind of criminals – double-crossing lying traitors! 'But you said we could . . .' they'll plead.

When I was young our entertainment consisted of a record player, a radio, a couple of jigsaw puzzles, a few dolls, and a dolls' house whose furniture I made myself from conkers, bits of old wood, and scraps from my mother's dressmaker. I really enjoyed making dolls' clothes; however, my enthusiasm faded one day when I left a needle sticking out of the carpet. Clever me – I knelt down on the needle, which went right into the bone of my shin. My parents could not remove it so I was carried, weeping copiously, to the emergency ward where they cut off my white sock and plucked out the offending object as I screamed my head off. I've been phobic about needles ever since, and I'm not much cop at sewing either.

When I visit my own children's homes, the mountains and mountains of toys astound me. When I gently suggest it might be generous to donate some to a children's hospital, outraged little faces stare back at me in horror. It's hard to change their minds when all babies are born behaving like little animals, demanding to be fed and watered when they want and yelling until they are. I think one essential way is to discipline them when they are young, and teach them to respect authority, whether it's their parents, grandparents, their teachers or policemen.

One of the things I was told when I was young, if my parents threatened to give me a good hiding or startled me in thunderous tones when I was about to do something dangerous, such as not looking before I crossed the street, was that they were doing it for my own good – and they were. I'm not expounding violence but young children don't know boundaries because their logical thought process is not yet formed. They have to be taught rudimentary forms of communication. Sternness and scolding, as guilty as you may feel about them, are essential to the formation of character. Feel-good, politically correct teachings risk creating a generation of kids with no concept of reality and can set them up for failure in the real world. Life is not fair – get used to it! In the real world, people expect results before handing out praise and they certainly don't give a fig about your self-esteem. You don't get jobs or promotions – you earn them. If you don't pay your bills, you go bankrupt; if you don't pay your mortgage, you lose your house; if you don't pay your taxes, you go to jail. A modicum of fear is necessary. And so is a modicum of challenge: the fad for telling kids how wonderful they are all the time poses the risk that they'll just drift through life not bothering to better themselves or work hard.

Children not only choose their meals now, but even what is bought, and it's an exceptional child who sits at a dining table finishing everything on the plate and doesn't watch TV at the same time. I see parents at supermarkets, airports and cinemas unable to control their rowdy children. We've given far too much credence to letting children 'express themselves', and it's time for the pendulum to swing the other way. Tolerance, compassion and discipline are all part of our value system, which is being eroded every day by giving instant gratification to our kids.

My mother always said to me, 'Start as you mean to go on.' Parenting, I believe, relies on constantly monitoring a set of consistent rules: regular bedtimes, regular meal-times always at the table, regular chores when the child is old enough and regular freedom once their homework and chores are accomplished. The more successful parents are the ones who seem to always have a watchful eye on their children's behaviour and address problem traits from the start – this is why parenting is said to be 'the toughest job you'll ever have'. And a fair amount of 'healthy contempt' is required, because constant attention creates unrealistic expectations, which in later life is unhealthy. In the end, though, there is no one certain method of parenting – just constancy, and faith that everything will turn out well.

If I ever said I was bored as a child, my parents retorted, 'People who are bored are boring!' and I've never forgotten it. According to my daughter Tara, to whom I repeated the same mantra, neither has she; it was ingrained in her brain, and she uses it on her own children who have far, far more to entertain themselves than she ever did.

Video games, Nintendo DSs (those handheld consoles which modern kids are rarely seen without), computers, iPods – it's a brave new world of technological wonders and amusements, yet they still whine that they're bored. Sometimes I tell my grandchildren THEY are boring – which goes down like a lead balloon.

But I'm amazed at the way their brains have adapted to cyberspace. When I asked twelve-year-old Miel how I could bid for something on eBay, she logged on in a fraction of the time it had taken me to work out exactly what on earth eBay was.

The dexterity of my grandchildren's fingers as they fly across the computer keys astounds me. I never learned to type, and although the majority of these young cyber kittens have never been taught either, they use their two index fingers and thumbs with astounding speed, and I've even seen two year olds playing with their parents' BlackBerries with ease. Their fingers seem shaped to accommodate the keys of most new-fangled technologies

– unlike mine. My own iPad has been commandeered by seven-year-old Ava Grace, who proceeded to download various albums with the latest techno-pop hits after visiting one of Saint Tropez's trendiest beaches, La Voile Rouge. 'Oh, this is a great song!' she chirped with excitement the next day as the relentless bass-line played at decibel proportions, making my hung-over brain melt like baked lasagna.

In my naivety, I imagined I was ahead of the game when Percy bought me this new technological marvel, but I have quickly been reminded of my limitations by the fish-to-water aptitudes of this younger generation. Even the way my grandchildren talk seems to be language from a different planet. Words like megabyte, gigs, Skype and blog sometimes sound double-dutch to me but roll off their tongues easily; however, while my grandson is still grappling with the basic concepts of reading, at the tender age of four I was reading Enid Blyton's *Famous Five* and at six was venturing into Dickens. There's no question that reading is one of life's great pleasures and it's sad that today so many kids are unable to read even at the age of twelve, which will certainly prevent them from getting a decent job when they're older.

But then why should they bother to learn to read when the magic of television and the Internet, with all its downloadable games and movies, is at their disposal twenty-four hours a day? How could a boring old book compare with that?

Plus it appears that the very act of learning to read has

been complicated by the new style of teaching that seems so odd to me: it's no longer a, b, c, but phonetically sounded in what appears to be a foreign dialect. Aah-bay-ka etc. I couldn't help them even if I wanted to.

As for manners, it seems that Ps and Qs are just another letter of the alphabet. As a child, I wouldn't have dreamed of leaving the table before my parents, not to mention leaving anything on my plate, because, as my mother would remind me, 'the children are starving in India'.

These words still ring in my brain, so that I feel a pang of guilt if I leave anything on my plate (portion control is the answer). But the pickiness of this generation is staggering! One grandchild is a vegetarian, one doesn't eat fish, one refuses anything green, another only wants meat, another only wants pasta with butter, and another only wants pasta with cheese. How do the parents cope?

I was not allowed sweets or chocolate during the day: 'They will rot your teeth,' said my mother. I had to go to bed at the same time every night, even at the height of British summer when it was still light at 10 p.m.

There's a chillingly pertinent scene in that Grand-Guignol biopic of Joan Crawford, *Mommie Dearest*. When her daughter refuses to finish her dinner, Crawford insists that it is served back to her at every mealtime and the poor child is forced to sit and stare at a congealing steak for days on end (not a technique I would advocate, but one that easily illustrates how times have changed).

The amount of food that is thrown into our rubbish

bins on a daily basis could feed a family of four in India for a week. As I silently tut-tut beneath my breath, raising my eyes to the ceiling in supplication, and wondering why the long-suffering parents of today seem to have no control, I ponder where my generation went wrong.

Or was it our children who went wrong, as they tried to revolt against the strict Victorian attitudes that I inherited and that our parents in turn inherited from theirs?

I was told what to wear until the age of fifteen – no two ways about it. My mother bought me simple dresses and sensible shoes from Clarks (so I now have perfect feet without corns or bunions!). My granddaughter has already suffered scarring to her knees from skidding across the carpet in high heels. There is no doubt that the fashion houses now cater to the very young when, in the past, there was no such thing as pre-teen and teenage fashion.

My children, who were born in the late sixties and seventies, were attired in matching outfits, gingham frocks and shorts, and I always insisted on socks and shoes. Today, looking at the clothes in the stores, you could be forgiven for thinking 'are these for tiny tots or tiny tarts?' Sequinned bikinis with hearts on the nether region, padded bras, sundresses cut out to the navel and lots of gothic black – for four year olds! The outfits are emblazoned with messages such as 'Born to shop' or 'Money is what parents are for', or 'I'm sexy'!

And magazines for young girls certainly exploit that.

Clothes aimed at pre-teens are blatantly sexy, and micro minis, crop tops and suggestive slogans on their T-shirts all contribute to the twisted notion that very young girls should be alluring – it's sick.

Sadly this trend seems to be becoming more prevalent as teenagers start experimenting with sex at an increasingly early age.

Youth is so fleeting that it's tragic to see younger and younger girls participating in behaviour that used to be reserved for adults only. But even more tragic is to see the pre-teen magazines encouraging this fast-track to adulthood by discussing sex so graphically and openly. Some of them even print articles about kissing and how to turn your boyfriend on!

In our holiday home we sometimes have after-dinner 'disco' parties in our living room where the children display an almost frightening propensity for adult dance moves, straight out of MTV or a Hannah Montana video. They are completely lacking in self-consciousness and when they perform 'It's Raining Men' with appropriate gestures, I wonder if they really understand what they are implying. It seems that today's children have all of the visual stimuli, but none of the understanding of what some songs mean.

As I watch them performing to the latest hits with so much confidence, charm and sophistication, I reflect on how I, as an insecure, shy child was never complimented by my parents, rarely told I was clever, pretty or talented, and basically told to shut up if I expressed any opinion.

Even so, I managed to overcome some of my shyness and lack of self-confidence. It was a gradual process exacerbated in my early twenties by the constant approbation of people at the studios telling me how wonderful I was and what a big star I was going to become. I never was much of a one for self-analysis and I'm also not good at blowing my own trumpet – but I'm getting better. If you haven't gained a certain amount of self-confidence, self-esteem and sophistication by the time you are in your forties then you must have gone through life with your eyes shut. As for acting, my grandmother encouraged me because of my great love of movies and movie stars.

Then at eighteen I was voted 'The Most Beautiful Girl in England' by an association of British photographers, but when Daddy was asked to comment he opined, 'Well, she's a nice-looking girl but nothing special.' And that is how I, and most of my generation of women were raised – that we were really just ordinary girls and should not deserve any special treatment or be treated any differently from anyone else.

Because of this we were inspired to work really hard to achieve success in our chosen field – we never had any concept of entitlement, which so many young people today feel.

If this attitude towards children seems harsh by today's standards, it's because it *was*. I do actually believe that if I had been given more praise and approbation, I would have become more successful and more knowledgeable in my business and financial affairs, which suffered not just from lack of encouragement but also because I was bad at and bored by maths. When I started earning significant money I just passed everything over to the *de rigueur* Los Angeles business managers and accountants and let them get on with it. I was good at making money, and *great* at spending it, but I was hopeless in between so, consequently, in the fallow periods after the prolific and well-paid work – seven years under contract to 20th Century Fox, nine years on *Dynasty* – I often found myself with little cash to show for my efforts.

If I had some of the business smarts and acumen of my alter-ego Alexis I would never have had to worry about money again. As a prime example, when *Dynasty* ended I was asked if I would sell my right to royalties in exchange for a lump sum of money. I was told by the producers of the ABC network, and stupidly believed without checking the facts, that serials such as ours never, ever go into reruns. What a joke! *Dynasty* finished twenty-three years ago and since then it has aired constantly in more than eighty countries over and over again. So much for not questioning authority. The producers and the networks have made billions of dollars whilst I and my fellow actors (who also sold their rights), receive our minimally contracted union sums, which in a good year amounts to about $500. Thrilling, huh?

Sadly I am not at all like Alexis Carrington Colby in that respect but thank God my grandkids are! I suppose one side-effect of getting their own way is the fact that they *have* learned to question authority, which is something I didn't learn until it was too late!

And so, as I wander around my French villa picking up soaking wet towels and bathing suits left in the wake of the kids, and avoiding tripping over the thousands of toys scattered around my normally pristine infinity pool, I have to admit that watching them jump and jiggle around, playing all afternoon, affords me some of the greatest pleasures of my already lucky life. It has to be said, kids may rule the roost, but who wants to be a peacock when their prancing is far more delightful and entertaining?

On Glamour: Which Never Sleeps

In 1955 I had just been cast in my first Hollywood movie, *The Girl in the Red Velvet Swing*. The part had been intended for Marilyn Monroe, but when she left Fox, fed up with the studio system, the role fell to me. At the age of twenty-one I was to play the most beautiful girl in New York.

After a day of rehearsing I walked into the cafeteria on the Fox studio lot for lunch one day wearing blue jeans, a T-shirt and – believe it or not – not a scrap of make-up.

As I walked through the cafe towards Richard Fleischer, the director of my movie, he saw me and threw his hands in the air.

'Oh my God,' he said. 'I can't look at you. You look hideous. You should always appear in public with full make-up, a nice dress and white gloves, otherwise you'll never get anywhere in this business.'

I was completely shocked. This was how young girls dressed, I thought. But when I was chatting to some of the other starlets later, they said I did look a bit scruffy and needed more glamour. So I decided I had to do something about my appearance and I'd better start smartening up my act. I realized that no one is born glamorous, but practically anyone can develop glamour.

So what is glamour? Is it what you wear? Certainly the clothes are important, of course, but in the end glamour isn't made up of low-cut dresses and sequins and feather boas. It has more to do with a particular aura, with grooming, with self-possession – and a touch of mystique.

Glamour is an almost mythical quality that I find difficult to accurately describe – and nor can anybody else, it seems. The dictionary defines it as 'sophisticated in style; alluring; attractive; bewitching; captivating; classy; dazzling; elegant; entrancing; glossy; seductive; magnetic; siren; smart . . .' Phew! That's a pretty broad sweep of a definition. And some stringent qualities to live up to. With expectations such as these, attaining glamour for some women must be akin to climbing Everest.

When I searched deeper I found the root meaning of the word, which is often ascribed to a variation of the Latin *grammatica*, which was used in the Middle Ages to mean scholarship or learning, especially regarding occult practices, which enabled the scholar to cast a spell. Thus, glamour is often associated with magic and the mystical! This is the definition I prefer – that changeable, evanescing, mystical practice that I revere appeals to me ''cause it's witchcraft', as Frank Sinatra sang.

There is no question that to be a glamorous woman is to be desirable, seductive and elegant. It's a complex word, most usually associated with movie stars, particularly from the era of the thirties and forties because they are memorable enough to be current and yet dead enough to be untouchable. These fabulous dames really possessed glamour in spades: Marlene Dietrich, Jean Harlow, Hedy Lamarr, Greta Garbo, Joan Crawford. The list is long, and looking at the smoky, soft-tinted photographs of these exciting women you can almost see and feel their allure, their power and, most particularly, their fierce individuality. No cookie cutter for these girls.

I was lucky enough to have been born with lots of dark hair and big eyes and was considered a pretty baby. I suppose I was quite cute because when I was six months old my mother had to put a sign on my pram that read: 'Please do not kiss me.'

I was 'discovered' as a photographic model while studying at RADA and was soon in demand. At eighteen, I was signed to the British film studio J. Arthur Rank where I played a succession of juvenile delinquents and young hookers, none of them in the least glamorous.

But I would glam up for premieres, borrowing clothes and sometimes a white mink stole from the studio wardrobe. At home, I was a blue-jeans-and-black-sweater kind of a girl, but my mother and my nine aunts, by contrast, were incredibly glamorous. They wouldn't have dreamed of stepping outside the house without wearing make-up and with their hair beautifully done. They would have considered it bad manners to do otherwise.

But then the forties and fifties were intensely glamorous decades, probably as a reaction to the previous constraints of wartime. Women looked up to film stars such as Hedy Lamarr, Betty Grable and Joan Crawford (after whom I was named). The clothes these stars wore on screen were often more important than the films themselves. So many women could sew then, and the films were like catwalks of fashion that they could replicate.

From the twenties to the sixties, ordinary women tried their best to look like their favourite stars. My mother aspired to Greer Garson and my Aunt Lalla to Marlene Dietrich. Then everything changed in the grungy seventies, before glamour made a big comeback in the eighties, helped in no small part by a certain television series called *Dynasty*.

By then I had gained a reputation as a woman who always made the best of herself, and who was determinedly glamorous, which was what I learned in the school of hard knocks – the Hollywood studio system.

After *The Girl in the Red Velvet Swing*, then *The Opposite Sex* with June Allyson, Leslie Nielsen and a bunch of glamour gals like Ann Miller, Dolores Gray and Joan Blondell, I became seriously interested in what I wore and I've never looked back. It was fantastically opulent, with fabulous clothes designed by Helen Rose – so my passion for beautiful clothes was born.

I was also lucky enough to have had Marilyn Monroe's make-up man, Alan 'Whitey' Snyder, showing me how to apply my make-up. (Sadly, just six years later, he was to make Marilyn up in her coffin.) Now, I can do my make-up in ten minutes, faster and better than anyone else I know. Some of my infallible cosmetic tips? Always keep your eyebrow pencils sharp as a pin, and never go outdoors without foundation to protect your skin, and lipstick, the most glam of cosmetics.

When I made *The Stud* and then *The Bitch* in the late seventies, I invented a look which I've stuck to more or less ever since: big hair, smoky eyes and bright lipstick. Also, I always do my own hair or wear wigs when I'm working or going to events where I'm likely to be photographed. I can't understand why so many women are averse to hairpieces or wigs. The amount of time they save is colossal because constant blow drying and straightening of hair is disastrous for it. But I do know that most long-haired actresses and models wear extensions.

So, when *Dynasty* and Alexis Carrington came along in the eighties, her look was already in place – it was mine. Sometimes, they tried to put me in little tweed jackets with pussycat bows, which just didn't work for the character.

Yves Saint Laurent and Pierre Cardin had just launched the big shoulder-padded look on the fashion world, and that felt right for Alexis. It seems it also caught the eye of Princess Diana, whose shoulder pads and hair were sometimes bigger than mine.

My dear friend Nolan Miller, the designer on the show, had dressed every star from Lana Turner to Betty Grable and Joan Crawford. He agreed that Alexis was a woman of the world, totally familiar with haute couture, so Nolan and I worked together and would go to the department stores Saks and Neiman Marcus every Saturday to pull designer clothes off the rails that we thought were very Alexis.

I usually needed ten costumes a week for *Dynasty*. In fact, there's an eleven-minute clip on YouTube of me walking in and out of rooms, always in a different outfit. I wore more outfits than I can count. Alexis Carrington Colby defined a decade that has become renowned for its unapologetic glamour, and I suppose it defined me, too.

I am bored with the constant criticism in the media of how ghastly eighties' fashions were. I think they were glorious. Thank God for the eighties say I. I only wish some of that glamour would return. How much more stylish and elegant most women looked then.

Admittedly with eighties style there were the unfortunate looks, like the one-piece jumpsuit, the over-developed footballers' shoulder pads and a plethora of gilt buttons on practically everything. However, the fashions that women wore were feminine, flattering and attractive. Sleek fitted suits accentuated the waist (which many women seem to no longer possess), softly draped wool, silk or jersey dresses worn over or just on the knee. Coco Chanel always believed that the knees were the ugliest part of the female anatomy and to that end, although she raised hemlines in the twenties, the longest part always stayed firmly on or below the bony joint. I still own several Chanel looks from the eighties and always feel elegant and modern even though they are vintage. And, of course, there was full hair – always a flattering frame for a face whatever the shape. Yes, it did become somewhat too big occasionally (think Melanie Griffith in *Working Girl* or Michelle Pfeiffer in *Married to the Mob*). But when I catch the odd photo of myself or other stars of eighties' TV, I'm often impressed by how good we all looked: groomed and well put together and frankly, m'dear, everyone unique and different from each other in their preferred style of hair and clothing. There I am posed on the steps of Alexis' Gulf Stream, wearing a pale grey jersey dress with a sweetheart neckline, accentuated by diamond clips, a matching cloche turban and gloves, enveloped by a grey cashmere cape edged in grey fox. I may look cool but it was 102° that day and the make-up man was hard at work with his portable mini-fan. And posing with the other stars of *Dynasty*, we are all impossibly tiny-waisted. I'm in a gold lamé sleeveless, backless and almost frontless evening gown, also split to the thigh. It was hard to act in this as parts of my body kept being revealed, which was against the strict TV censorship of the eighties.

In the eighties the sleeve was a major feature of most evening gowns. It was often big and puffy but usually stunningly elegant, thus covering up those bits that most women over forty want to cover. To meet the Queen Mother at a royal premiere, I sported a shocking-pink satin number adorned with three massive bows on each shoulder. When I turned sideways, my face was completely hidden. There's a boring sameness about eveningwear today, unless of course it's couture, boned and fitted to the nth degree. Alexander McQueen was a brilliant designer who learned his craft working in Savile Row where beautiful bespoke suits for men were made. His successor Sarah Burton made the stunning wedding dress for Kate Middleton truly a work of art. It seems to have inspired other designers today to make clothes that fit a woman's body and don't just hang like a sack.

Joan Crawford once said: 'I feel I owe it to my public always to look good. When you're young, you can get away with the careless, ungroomed look. But to not bother with grooming over the age of forty is a mistake.' And as the High Priestess of Glamour, Joan should know.

On programmes such as *The Jeremy Kyle Show*, you wonder what the world is coming to. Those stringy-haired, tattooed women could use a little glamour in their lives (although it would be a challenge for the ones who are very overweight).

It's difficult for women to get inspiration today and I find it hard to think of more than four or five actresses who epitomize glamour. Certainly, they manage it on the red carpet or in a movie role. It's quite easy to achieve with a team of stylists, designers, personal trainers, beauticians, hairdressers, jewellers and all the others who help to create that magic illusion. But, sadly, just like Cinderella after the ball, most of the stars and starlets go back to their jeans and T-shirts the next day, because they don't realize that part of being glamorous means that you should try to look good *all the time*.

This does not mean you have to walk your dog on the beach in wedges and beach loungewear – glamour is also sensible. I have seen glamorous women make the oldest clothes look like couture because they know what looks good on them and how to carry it off. Too many times women simply put clothes on, rather than wear them. Bump into a Hollywood actress on a plane or at a restaurant and she will usually lack that magic that enthralls us. And, in fairness, who can be glamorous *all the time* when, like many women today, they've spent the last two decades following the defiant rebellion against glamour and so have forgotten what looks good on them and how to achieve it. For example, many women today don't wear make-up because they don't think they need it. And also because they are simply too petrified to wear it and have no idea how to apply it.

How sad this is.

Through the ages women have always emulated other women whose allure and style keep raising our expectations and push us harder 'not to let the side down'. In the eighteenth century, Queen Marie Antoinette was the epitome of glamour and her court slavishly copied her gowns and hairstyles. Cleopatra also stands out as an epitome of ageless beauty, beguiling not only those of her day, but us as well. And when Jackie Kennedy and Princess Diana were at the height of their popularity there were lookalikes all over the world striving to capture their particular brand of glamour. It was the same for men. The age of the dandy was really not so long ago.

Nowadays it seems everyone imitates famous role models who dress down rather than up, or the unattainably thin and unhealthily anorexic models. And don't get me started on piercings and tattoos – imagine what those will look like the older you become.

It is possible to be glamorous without all the tricks of special lighting, couture gowns and self-appointed 'stylists' (who mostly seem to be men who don't have a clue what flatters real women). Without meaning to blow my own horn – if I can shop and dress myself and do my own make-up and hair without the help of stylists and personal attendants and still manage to attain praise for my style, then there is nothing to stop you from doing the same. All you need to do is learn what looks good on you and focus on your individual style. The Duchess of Cambridge is a case in point – extremely glamorous yet she styles herself and dresses brilliantly.

With classic outfits, excellent grooming and a strong sense of self, practically any woman can become, if not a charismatic Hollywood goddess, then attractive and worthy of admiration and some envy for her unique style. I've stressed how important grooming is – messy hair, shiny, make-up-less faces, bulging tummies and sloppy clothes are the antithesis of beauty. This so-called 'natural' look is just an excuse to be lazy and undisciplined. It is not understated – because understated can also be extremely glamorous.

I remember the first time I met Grace Kelly – it was when she was already the Princess of Monaco. She was one of the most glamorous, yet understated, women I've ever met. She was sitting by the swimming pool at David Niven's house in Cap Ferrat. Her immaculate blond hair was shining, yet in a classically subdued style. She wore a pale blue cashmere twin set, a pleated grey skirt and a string of pearls. She was simply yet elegantly dressed and confident about herself.

Glamour is not only about what you wear – it is also about your personality. Glamorous women seem to share something extraordinarily attractive that comes from inside. It could be a serene, ethereal quality, a fiery, independent brassiness or a regal bearing, but whatever it may be, glamorous women possess it in spades.

Women such as Grace Kelly or Ava Gardner weren't perfect, they had flaws like the rest of us, but they knew enough about how to present themselves to appear flawless.

Being glamorous doesn't mean being supermodel tall either. Many of the golden-era screen sirens were under 5ft 2in., and since regular exercise such as Pilates or going to the gym were practically unheard of those days, many had a much softer body shape than what is admired today. I don't remember anyone every talking about Marlene Dietrich's abs. Or Marilyn Monroe's biceps . . .

What these women knew about was the art of disguise, so that any imperfections – perceived or real – would fade into the background of the overall picture of poise and personality. For glamour, as I already told you, is a wizards' brew of illusion and artifice that intoxicates and bewitches.

Glamorous skin

I've always been sceptical about the so-called miracle creams that proliferate on the overdone cosmetic counters of major department stores worldwide. I raise an even more cynical eyebrow when I see glossy magazine or TV ads of gorgeous twenty-something models recommending and extolling the virtues of anti-ageing creams, or over-fifty actresses who have had a lot of 'work' done but still say they owe it all to some cream.

Who do they think they're kidding? Are the big cosmetic companies convinced that the average woman is deluded enough to believe the preposterous claims in their advertising? Or is it just that they think that sex sells everything today and that twenty year olds are more glamorous than forty year olds (and up), so let's show pure youthful beauty in our ads and let the poor fool who buys the product think that she too could look like the young model if she used the product? And to add insult to injury, these baby-faced models are 'beauty washed' and photo-shopped, meaning the photos are retouched until their faces and skin have the perfection only possible in a two year old.

What sane woman is going to believe that a certain lotion is going to 'refine, renew and transform your skin in ten minutes'? Or that 'it melts luxuriously into your skin and creates a younger, revitalized look instantly'? The advertising agencies must be laughing their heads off, and all the way to the banks, because these products do sell – and women often do believe that buying these 'miracle' products – at fifty or sixty pounds a pop, if not more – is going to change their looks, if not their lives.

I find it really rather sad to see a lady earnestly discussing with the make-up 'expert' at the beauty counter how a particular cream is going to erase the forty years of hard living etched on her face.

The ageing process of the skin is attributable to so many factors – the pollutants skin has to cope with, air conditioning, heating, general exposure to the sun, wind and the elements, not to mention the various toxins we put into our body through the food we eat and the beverages we drink. We need to think about these things too when we want skin and figures as perfect as possible.

Take anti-cellulite creams: these are one of the great myths perpetuated by the modern cosmetic industry. The only way to reduce cellulite is to radically banish junk and fatty food from your diet, take copious amounts of fish oil and other supplements and, yes, dear reader, exercise, exercise, exercise until your derriere starts to show results. We all know what a drag that can be, but there's no way around the drudgery of reality, and cellulite is seriously unglamorous.

We live in a quick-fix society where we need instant gratification for everything. Too fat? Get lipo-sucked. Stringy hair? Glue on those extensions. Wrinkles and lines? Head to the beauty counter or Botox clinic. It's all a billion-pound con foisted upon insecure women by canny big-business conglomerates.

The Advertising Standards Authority (ASA) – the watchdog that protects the public against false claims, ruled against one of these companies recently. The company claimed its anti-cellulite contouring serum could not only destroy cellulite, but with its exclusive ingredients could actually 'melt away' the fatty look of the stuff. The ASA concluded the ads were misleading and made medical claims they could not substantiate. As a result, they ordered a recall of all the products.

Now, please don't get the impression that I'm against any skin-protecting beauty product ever produced. *Au contraire!* Since my early teens my glamorous mother, aunts and even my grandmother encouraged me to take care of my skin by proper cleansing, moisturizing and protecting. This was long before the sophisticated products available today that boast they can do everything except whistle Dixie. I used the simplest products – cold cream, baby oil, Vaseline, rose water – all the generic skin products available at the local chemist. My foundation was then a low-priced brand that I'd usually buy from Woolworth's. Mummy didn't let me have too many sweets or chocolates and made me eat all my greens. She also insisted on a teaspoon of cod liver oil each day – ugh! But it worked for Granny, Mummy and my aunts, and it worked for me.

There's something else though that's vitally important to glamorous-looking skin: sun protection. Even though I was making a life-long commitment to skin care, I still used to bake my face and my body in the sun at every possible opportunity, until one day, my glamorous friend Cappy Yordan (whose skin at thirty was like porcelain) berated me for my sunbathing habits.

'Do you want to look like them when you're forty?' She indicated a posse of darkly tanned lizard-like women lapping up the sun by the Beverly Hills Hotel pool.

'God, no, that couldn't happen to me,' I laughed, with all the cockiness of a twenty year old.

'It certainly will if you don't quit putting your face in the sun,' said Cappy sternly. 'Once you get sun damage, there's absolutely nothing you can do to get rid of it, so stop now or you'll regret it for ever.'

I looked at her lovely skin and decided I should heed her advice. Since then I have been fanatical about protecting my face, if not my body, against the sun's rays in summer and winter. After moisturizing, I slap on a sunscreen-enhanced foundation, which protects skin far more efficiently than any of the so-called 'miracle creams' and I always wear a hat or a cap because even on the darkest of days the sun's rays can penetrate through the clouds and cause damage.

That's my miracle 'cream' for good skin, and many of my girlfriends who have followed the same advice still look amazingly good. I strongly believe in protecting first rather than shutting the barn door after the horse has bolted. With the harmful UVAs and UVBs in the environment, it is essential to start your regime as soon as possible if you want to stave off the ageing process and look glamorous well into later life.

It is essential to always put something moisturizing on your face and then, with foundation on top, you will avoid much of the wear and tear that ageing brings. I'm often amazed when some lined, red-faced, blotchy-skinned woman proudly announces that she's never allowed an ounce of make-up touch her face. Well, bully for you, ma'am, if you want to go to the grave looking like Dracula's grandma, but if you want to look glamorous, then start putting on the make-up.

Some media witches have mocked me for always wearing make-up, but they should take note, for I can absolutely assure them that if you take two women over fifty, one of whom has always protected her face with foundation and one of whom has never done anything other than wash with soap and water, guess which one will have the best skin? And not just slightly less lined, but miles and miles better with skin that looks twenty years younger and infinitely more glamorous. Teach your children also: it's never too early to start.

How to dress

It's every woman's day-mare: what to wear? Does my bum look big in this? Do I look fat?

I've always maintained that there is a fine line between a daring, sexy older woman and mutton dressed as lamb. Millions of women go through this angst every day, particularly after they've flicked through the glossies and seen the glamorously turned out yet oh-so-casual-looking actresses and models that grace the pages. But that effortless look worn by the eternally sleek Naomi Campbell or the petite but perfectly proportioned Kate Moss and dozens of others does not come easy.

First of all, magazine models and most actresses preparing for a shoot or a glamorous premiere have stylists to coordinate their outfits, to match a certain top with the right belt, with that chic but droopy jacket. During a shoot the stylist has a rack of hundreds of items of clothing from the crème de la crème of designers, which enables her to get the perfect look. And guess what? Some of the clothes don't even look good on these goddesses. The clothes are pinned and tucked up strategically out of sight of the camera lens, or sometimes manipulated in such a way – using props like fans and great lighting – that they look great. It's not easy, and it's far different from how it was in previous decades.

Women today are taller and bigger that they were fifty,

forty and even twenty years ago, and the difference between the models and the average woman is much more marked. In the fifties the average woman was 5ft 2in, had a 27-inch waist, and weighed around 8½ stone, and so did the average clothes model.

Most women wearing the 'New Look', Christian Dior's post-war, reactionary and revolutionary style of long skirt, crinoline and a tightly cinched-in waist with a jacket or dress looked stylish. The style was flattering but you had to have an hourglass figure, which many women did actually achieve thanks to corsetry. Study old photos of relatives from the forties or fifties and you'll notice how practically everyone looked glamorous and had made an effort to look good, even those who may not have had the perfect figure.

Today, because we all eat far too much, the average woman is 5ft 4in., has a 34-inch waist and weighs about 11 stone whereas the average model is required to be at least 5ft 8in. and have measurements of 34-24-34. Even the slimmest of girls don't have a waist proportionately ten inches smaller than their bust or hips. With this kind of disparity, how would the average woman be able to fit into the clothes worn by the models in the fashion magazines?

When I was in *Dynasty*, we were dressed in eighties fashions not dissimilar from those of the forties and fifties: tight jackets and skirts and padded shoulders, which make the waist look smaller. If you didn't have the contours you could 'fake' them with corsetry, padded bras and fine tailoring. However, in the more Spartan nineties and noughties, the media and fashionistas rebelled against and mocked eighties' fashion, but without giving us much of anything to take its place. What we were given instead was saggy, baggy and bland, such as the 'LBD' – made of cheap fabric, shapeless and all black.

I'm happy to say that more glamorous clothes can now be found, even on the high street, and current collections feature a more tailored and fitted look than in recent years. Haute couture, however, remains the domain for those millionaires who are at least 5ft 8in. and no more than 120lb, so if you crave that look and aren't a model-sized millionaire, then *fuggedaboudit!*

There are many other ways to look stylish and glamorous at any age, just don't make the mistake of trying to look like anyone in fashion, showbiz, or the media. You are an individual, just as they are, and you need to play up your best features and play down your not-so-good ones. That's what the glam queens of Hollywood always did!

A few more specifics:
Invest in an all-in-one Spanx-type undergarment. This deceptively simple structure is a masterpiece of engineering. It cleverly wraps around the diaphragm, hips and waist to hold in all those wobbly bits, thus showing off your glamorous sexy curves. And let's face it, all women do, or should, have curves, because who wants to look like a boy, even though that seems to be the shape far too

many top designers crave in their clothes-hanger figured models.

I had to laugh recently when I read in a fashion magazine: 'Big up your look for fall with a billowy skirt, dress or jacket.' Billowy only suits willowy, and if you're under 5ft 7in. you'll look like a mushroom, or worse still a tent at Glastonbury. Full skirts are seriously unflattering, (remember Princess Beatrice at the Royal Wedding?) and the only exception I make is the gypsy skirt, which I have been wearing for years and actually looks quite glam on most sized women. As for blousy tops cinched in with a belt, that is also a look doomed to failure. You'll just come off resembling a pup-tent with a belt.

If you're beyond your teenage years micro-mini skirts are out, as are skirts or trousers that end below the belly button. There is nothing more unsightly than a great gob of belly fat falling over your belt for all the world to mock – it's bad enough on a teenager, but downright frightful on anyone over forty. Crop tops and little sleeveless dresses belong to your daughter's generation.

As for tattoos or piercing anywhere (except for the earlobes) leave them for the bikers and shaven headed yobbos, as there is nothing more unglamorous.

Frankly, little slip dresses on anyone over a size ten are seriously unflattering. Not only do they show every bulge, but most of them are so cheaply made that they look terribly tacky. As gorgeous as Nicole Kidman is, I've seen photos of her looking distinctly below par in a slip dress. Even if you have a great figure, the slip dress does nothing for it, and since they're usually made with the same width of fabric in the bust, waist and hips, it makes most women look like a flowered ironing board.

In bright or pastel colours, polo necks make anyone with a bust size of more than 36B resemble a stuffed sausage. The only colour to wear in a polo (or a turtleneck) is black. In fact, black is the magic colour. Nothing is more flattering, except for white. Black takes pounds off any figure, makes your bum and waist look smaller, and is (nearly) always chic. When I'm having a 'fat day', it's straight to the black jacket (tailored), skirt or trousers and, do not pass go, black tights, which I'm happy to say are also having a comeback. A touch of white near the neckline, a collar or a flower, is a slam-dunk youthful look.

Another unglamorous look is bare legs in winter. Unless yours are really toned, tanned and veinless, leave the naked pins to those idiotic or young enough not to care about freezing to death. There is nothing more elegant in winter than dark tights worn with matching knee length boots and a belted trench coat.

Strangely enough, belted topcoats or tailored jackets do not make you look heavier. On the contrary, the more tailored the look, the sleeker you appear and by consequence 'thinner' (or at least more in proportion and put together). This is particularly true if the coat is three-quarter length. Certainly Peter Sellers, even as the buffoon Clouseau in the *Pink Panther*, managed to look quite chic in his belted Burberry. Knee-length coats, by contrast, and unless worn with trousers, are unflattering and often look cheap.

One of the most flattering current styles is the classic Diane von Furstenberg wrap dress. All sorts of dresses are having a major comeback, as women discover the simple joys of putting on just one garment in the morning and not agonizing about matching the trousers and the top to the cardigan, which can often end up looking a mess anyway. But I think the Diane von Furstenberg dress is by far the best. I've had them made in many colours and fabrics, and the shape is extremely flattering for all figures. It's a glamorous look without striving for it. Another glamorous and easy-to-wear look is the 'Jackie-O' look that has made a comeback with the character Bree in *Desperate Housewives* and on the Duchess of Cambridge. So long as the skirt is pencil thin and hits the knee and the top or cardigan are well fitted, it can look fabulous.

Waistcoats are another essential for a casual, yet put-together effect. I've been wearing them for years, long before the recent fad was thrust upon us. A waistcoat is an extremely versatile accessory, as it can be worn over anything (other than a coat). It has the added benefit of disguising your waistline, a blessing for most of us, while at the same time creating the visual effect of having a waist by separating the bottom half from the top half of your body. Whether in silk or suede, you can wear them summer or winter and they always looks right. The classic three-piece suit in black or white is never out of place and can be worn dressed down for the office or up for an evening out. Just change the accessories and you'll look truly glam.

Hats have long been a favourite accessory of mine, and are another glamorous essential. I'm not talking about the silly mad-hatter numbers we laugh about at Ascot. I'm talking about fedoras, berets, stetsons or baker-boy caps, or even the ubiquitous fascinators, which are timeless and classics. All are face enhancing – but you must try on many to find the most flattering shape. Hats are particularly glamorous if worn with confident élan. If any-one makes fun of you in a hat, just fix them with a disdainful expression and say, 'It keeps the sun off my face'.

Most ankle-strap shoes are seriously unattractive and don't even look good on young girls. Sure, those magazine layouts with a gorgeous model seductively raising a toned leg in laced up stilettos make you want to buy them, but they won't work on a real-life woman. Don't attempt any kind of ankle adornment. Only Joan

Crawford could get away with that kind of fetish footwear, and although in photos it looks glamorous, it's faintly ridiculous today.

Apart from cutting the line of the leg, ankle straps also cut off the circulation. Try dancing in them – your feet will look like a pair of overdone hot dogs afterwards. Here again classic is best and nothing looks better than black court shoes with heels and black tights or the famous Chanel courts, two-tone beige with black toecaps. They are never out of fashion and always look fabulous. You won't feel good if your feet hurt. A wince is never a winning look.

So-called designer handbags are useless, and most of them are ugly and faddish, not to mention overpriced. Anna Wintour, the powerful and chic editor of US *Vogue* rarely ever carries a bag, but for most of us it's essential. Pared down and sleek is always best. For evening try a simple clutch with enough room for compact, lippie, cash, keys and phone. It can be leather, suede, satin or beaded, in a simple colour and will look good with everything. For daytime, those enormous bags with 900 different compartments for everything including the kitchen sink are a nightmare because you stuff far too much in them and can never find anything when you need it. I still love my classic Chanel shoulder chain bags, and I wore them even when they weren't in style because they are classic. I also like a simple medium-sized tote in which you can look quickly and see everything at a glance. As long as you keep your wallet in a zippered compartment to avoid pickpockets, life can be infinitely easier.

When I browse through the latest issues of the fashion magazines I'm appalled at how fussy and overdone all these bags are, with their bits and bobs hanging off them for no good reason, and their silly padlocked and fiddly compartments that totally distract from a chic glamorous appearance.

Any garment with too many frills, buttons or bows is unglamorous and there are far too many of them around nowadays. I still own and wear classic tweed, Chanel and YSL jackets and skirts from years ago and I wouldn't think of getting rid of them for some trendy fussy look that's all the rage. Less is more for true elegance and although a ton of chains, pendants and dangly scarves and bracelets may look cute on a young model, they usually look distinctly overdone. When I finish dressing and accessorizing, I usually look in the mirror long and hard then end up removing something. Whether it's a belt, bracelet or a bauble, less is always more.

Don't be afraid to experiment with colour, particularly with jewel colours such as crimson, purple and emerald. These are rich and glamorous and, like black and white, more flattering than beige, brown, grey or greige. But don't overdo the purple and orange combination as Cheryl Cole did recently.

A v-neck is the most attractive style whatever your size and, since most women's shoulders are also attractive, off-the-shoulder tops are glamorous for evening. I have a ton of them and it's my favourite evening look. You want people to look at *you* and not at what you're wearing, so keep it simple, stylish but not faddish and do collect classic signature pieces.

If you must wear jeans, which are rarely glamorous on women over forty, wear them dark blue or black, well fitted, and paired with black polo-necks or t-shirts and a classically cut jacket.

I haven't really liked jeans for years – probably because their obsequiousness has become terribly boring. Do people *really* want to conform to looking just like everyone else? Is it laziness or lack of money that puts vast swathes of the UK and US populations into identical denim? Actually, these denim pieces are not all identical by any means. There are hundreds of different categories of jeans nowadays: baggy, tight, low-rise, high-rise, boot-cut, flared and those dreadful hipsters, which often fall so low they show acres of ugly 'builders' cleavage'. But don't wear the high-waisted Simon Cowell-type trousers, which gives the wearer the faint look of being strangulated, or the hang-low long shorts with frayed hems which will make you look like a vagrant.

Of course denim is hard-wearing and practical, but most chic women wouldn't be caught dead in them.

When I wear jeans that are form-fitting, I find myself constantly rearranging them in the mid-section and below because they just feel really uncomfortable. Then again, they look horrible if they are easy and loose – I feel I look like Michelin man, particularly if I'm also wearing a sweater.

The first time I ever saw a woman wearing blue jeans was in *Summer Stock* – an American collegiate movie-musical in glorious Technicolor. All the girls were in full tightly waisted dirndl skirts with petticoats and white bobby socks, except for one tomboy-type with attitude who wore sassy, high-waisted blue jeans rolled up to mid-calf. As an impressionable teenager, this actress epitomized to me the modern emancipated woman, and the rolled-up denims emphasized her desire not to conform to the sweet June Allyson collars and little white-gloved look of the majority of her generation.

Fashion for teenagers was non-existent in the early fifties. Girls still wore mini-versions of their mothers' drab frocks or cardigan sets and the word 'teenager' was a new phenomenon somewhat disapproved of by a generation brought up by the credo that children should be 'seen and not heard'. Never one to abide by these rules myself, I begged my mother to buy some blue jeans for me, which she reluctantly agreed to do, and then hissed to my father, 'Why does Joan want to wear those ugly trousers? They look awful.'

But ever persuasive, off we traipsed to the usual shops: Selfridges, John Lewis, Bourne & Hollingsworth, in search of teenage-type jeans, but they were nowhere to be found. Then someone at RADA, where I was a student at the time, suggested buying the smallest men's-size jeans and shrinking them to fit. I discovered a shop on Tottenham Court Road that specialized in sportswear for men, but the smallest size was still far too big for me.

Undaunted I bought them with my saved-up pocket money and, back home, sat in a boiling hot bath for over an hour wearing the jeans. I had been advised they would shrink to fit my body and what do you know? It worked! When I rolled them up at the cuff and swanned around proudly at RADA showing off to all my envious classmates, I was one of a kind because no one else had them.

I loved those jeans and wore them endlessly, until they finally dropped off me, but the novelty factor was that I was just one of very few girls who actually possessed American-style blue jeans, which gave me much teenage cachet. On a riverboat shuffle, I wore them with a tartan shirt and was photographed by *Picture Post*, the then equivalent of *Hello!* magazine, and was described as the 'girl who dresses très-jazz' (I was completely unknown at the time.)

Fast forward a few decades and suddenly there is nothing novel or counter-culture in wearing a pair of blue jeans: it's like wearing a uniform. Today so many people wear jeans all the time that most people have zero individuality from the waist down. They are just a sea of blue-legged homogeny, in different shapes and sizes . . . and what shapes and sizes there are!

I rarely see anyone, male or female, wearing jeans that flatter them in any way whatsoever, with the exception of stick thin models and actresses. Fat people just look fatter in them, particularly the low-rise type which leaves a mass of blubber hanging over the belt. It amazes me to see with what aplomb some people flaunt themselves in fat-enhancing jeans – it's even more hideous when the *avoirdupois* is adorned with various colourful tattoos. Tiny people with thin legs tend to look like giant spiders when they wear those so-called skinny jeans so beloved of our magazine fashion editors in the glossy style bibles. In their tight bum-enhancing garments many actresses and models look cute from the waist up but completely conformist from the waist down.

Face it – jeans are just not comfortable. I own about six pairs of different coloured jeans, which, when I occasionally decide to wear them, end up being way down on the comfort factor, and they never look that good either. Even though I'm reasonably thin below the belt, I honestly don't like how I look in jeans and I think this holds true for many women *d'un age certain*.

It astounds me to hear some of my friends talking about their designer jeans that cost upwards of £500 – what a waste of money! I see little difference between these and the knock-offs that abound in the high street. I bought a pair of the latter recently and wore them tucked into boots, with a leather jacket for a low-key shopping trip to a mall in West Hollywood. I thought I would be quite indistinguishable from the rest of the crowd there, until a few days later I saw my picture in the *Daily Mail*. I had been 'outed' by a paparazzo. Great disguise, that was.

I won't give up wearing jeans altogether, since I've become quite fond of that particular pair, which are more comfortable and stylish than the others, but I do carefully choose the places where I'll wear them. For example, in Saint Tropez, where we spend most of the summer, I wear white jeans to the market or shopping at the grocery store, and if it's really cold, on a boat. When I'm filming, I'll throw on a pair in the early morning, but in general, I will only wear jeans for the purpose they were originally designed for – functionality. I wouldn't dream of wearing jeans to any of the restaurants I frequent; however, I did wear them recently on a movie-and-dinner evening with Percy, my daughter Tara and her two children in Weston-super-Mare. Since there was nowhere open to eat after the movie had finished, we hit the local McDonald's, where several of the clientele appeared shocked to see me dining there. But I think it was probably me in blue jeans that surprised them most.

Soon after I made the slightly risqué movie *The Stud*, Philip Green contacted me about launching my own line of blue jeans. I met Mr Green – then known in the rag trade as 'The Bond Street Bandit' and now Sir Philip the billionaire owner of Topshop – in his shop in Conduit

Street, where he sold designer clothes from previous seasons. Even then he had enormous entrepreneurial spirit. I thought it was an interesting proposal, as designer jeans were not as common then as they are now. So the 'Joan Collins Jeans' line was launched, and off I went to flog 'em in various department stores in the provinces. They created quite a stir, as I must admit they were extremely well cut and flattering. They were made of dark blue denim and fitted perfectly in all the right places. Sadly, however, the line didn't last, so a rare pair of 'JC Jeans' now apparently goes for a pretty penny on eBay.

What else can denim be used for now? Other than jeans in every colour under the sun, it is now made into bags, boots, corsets, bracelets, cushions, baby clothes – anything one can possibly imagine. Fashion editors have even decreed that one can wear denim top-to-toe without looking naff, but they are at least better than arguably the greatest fashion monstrosity ever – the nylon shell suit!

I discovered long ago that, if you look good, you feel good. Don't believe any woman who says she doesn't like a compliment. If I'm walking through a store or into a restaurant and someone says I look great, it lifts my spirits.

Not long ago, I had a heavy cold and cough and was looking like the wrath of God. Catching sight of myself in the mirror, slopping around bare-faced in a dressing gown with messy hair made me feel even worse. After three days at home, I had to go out for several long-standing appointments, and, as I put on my make-up and dressed in a glamorous outfit, I could feel myself getting better.

So the message is clear, girls. Glamour really is good for you.

On Modern-day Travel: Come Fly with Me; it's Hell!

The first time I ever went on a plane was when I was a teenager. My mother took my younger sister, brother and I to Dinard on the northern coast of France. We were all immensely excited by the prospect of this glamorous trip and spent many weeks mulling over our outfits: not just what to wear on holiday but more importantly what to wear on the two-hour flight. This was the fifties and women (and men) cared a great deal about how they looked. My mother chose an elegant grey fitted skirt-suit with a cream blouse and a strand of pearls. She had had her hair freshly done the previous day and looked band-box beautiful.

My little brother, Bill, was attired in navy-blue shorts, a matching blazer and white ankle socks. Sister Jackie wore a trendy pair of blue capris with a pretty twinset; and I wore my best outfit, a full 'New Look' type skirt in felt appliquéd with small poodles. I had made it myself at school (yes, we had sewing lessons then!) and was inordinately proud of it. I also wore a fitted angora bolero.

We thought we all looked pretty well turned out when we arrived at London airport. Then looking around the small terminal, I realized that everyone else was also dressed to the nines. All the women were coiffured, manicured and made-up, and they wore attractive summer dresses or well-cut slack combos. The men were grey-flannelled and tweed-jacketed, many of them in ties, and there was a palpable air of anticipation and excitement.

What a contrast to today when the costume du jour for the traveller is to dress down as tattily and casually as possible, and to look stressed and haggard.

When I flew to Hollywood in the mid-fifties I was dressed to kill in a tight-fitting red dress and a full length brown mink coat, which was so heavy that I couldn't possibly carry it. In fact I always dress for travel as the sloppy tracksuit look doesn't quite do it for me. (The young Duchess of Cambridge dressed perfectly for her Canadian trip: a sleek blue blazer and Roland Mouret dress.)

The worst dressed traveller I ever had the misfortune to sit next to was in shorts yet shoeless and shirtless – not even a singlet, and we were in boiling-hot Acapulco! I asked the flight attendant gently if I could be moved, but there were no empty seats. Then I suggested that my neighbour put something on but the attendant said there was no dress code on the airline – really! I suppose he could have worn a jockstrap and it would have sufficed. The sweat poured off the guy as we flew to LA, and as he wasn't wearing any deodorant I needed a good blast of smelling salts when we arrived. It goes without saying that I never took that airline again.

'Pack Light!' 'Capsule Wardrobe!' These phrases strike fear into the heart of a dedicated shopper. Ever since I began to divide my time between London and the US I've been compelled to travel like some ghastly packhorse toting dozens of assorted suitcases with my, admittedly, prodigious amounts of clothes, accessories, books, CDs, DVDs and occasionally the odd household chattel from one residence to another – I realize that I garner little pity but *c'est ma vie*.

Some people think I'm mad to go through this procedure a couple of times a year but far from being a chore I actually enjoy it and I'm lucky to have my three secret weapons. Number one is First Luggage, a great company that picks up the cases from one home or hotel or wherever I am and magically whisks them to the next port of call. Secondly there are my two wonderful ladies who professionally pack all the things I've laid, or rather *chucked*, out on the bed, sofa, chairs, my husband or any surface available at the moment. Yvonne in the US has been packing my bags for twenty-five years and Chrissie has been doing the same in London for the past ten.

When I was touring *Private Lives* in the US in the nineties and schlepping from one climatic zone to another and desperately stuffing everything from swimsuits to raincoats in a haphazard manner, my then PR, Chen San, after seeing my frustration at the god-awful lack of organization, took pity and decided to pack for me. When I protested and told her that was not her job, she waved me away with an airy, 'I always did this for Liz.' I was aware that Elizabeth Taylor had always beaten me in the overweight luggage department, so my packing would be a doddle by comparison. I happily let Chen deal with the mountains of tissue paper that she 'always used for Liz', so my garments were organized and pristine for the rest of the tour. Now I always place tissue paper between garments when I pack as it prevents creases; I stuff my shoes with it and I fold my jackets and coats inside out.

My luggage is at least twenty years old, and mostly Vuitton, which holds up reasonably well on the rough and tumble of the carousel and from being thrown about by baggage handlers. But try taking a piece back to the Vuitton store for a little nip and tuck and you'll end up paying almost as much as for a new piece of luggage. I don't think the new models are as roomy and sturdy as my old ones, so I've discovered yet another secret weapon

– a terrific little repair man in West Hollywood who can fix absolutely anything in leather.

One of the main reasons I now send my luggage ahead most of the time is to avoid being present during the dreaded customs search. I'm religious about declaring what I've bought and fortunately have never had any trouble . . . except for one ghastly experience. Returning to the US from Paris after filming *Sins* there for three months, I had about thirty pieces of luggage with me. Mind you, I was also travelling with my eleven-year-old daughter, her nanny and my personal assistant, so their bags accounted for some of the excess as well. Valentino had created some glorious outfits for the film and these I had packed carefully myself and instructed the concierge to send them to my house in the South of France. Well, *somebody* goofed big time because, as I blithely handed the officer my customs card declaring a few things I had purchased, he stopped me and demanded I open up some of my cases. To my horror, the first case he opened contained several hardly worn Valentino gowns, which he took out and examined one by one.

'But they were supposed to stay in France,' I stammered, 'the concierge made a mistake!' But Mr Officious cared naught for my protestations of innocence. Every suitcase was opened and minutely examined: underwear, nightgowns, bras and knickers were strewn about as people passed by curiously glancing at me while I was cross-questioned severely. Since this was during the height of *Dynasty* fever, several fellow passengers whipped out their cameras and snapped me looking woeful and dishevelled as I vainly protested my innocence. After three hours of hell they finally believed me and let me go but not before they had examined every single item. I felt as if I'd been a criminal and in fact I was put on a Federal list for suspected smugglers so that every time I entered the US for the next five years my luggage was thoroughly searched.

The only time I did take a 'capsule' wardrobe was for a modelling gig in South Africa. The photographer (and erstwhile friend) who booked it had insisted that I only take a carry-on bag as the photo shoot was in a safari camp accessible exclusively by small plane from Johannesburg, and so weight distribution was crucial. Grumbling all the way I dutifully, but reluctantly, complied, packing into a tiny bag only four suitable outfits that I hoped would look diverse enough for the shoot.

I arrived at the airport and met the photographer, who was carrying two huge suitcases. 'Is that equipment?' I asked. 'No, that is,' she said as she pointed to a small bag. 'The rest are my safari clothes.'

I was annoyed to say the least and demanded, 'How come? Why are you taking all of that? *I'm* the model!' She then became quite stroppy and we had a row, which ended up with us not speaking to each other for a while.

So, beware of packing light – not only can it exhaust you from trying to figure out what you can get into a small bag, but it can seriously damage your friendships!

*

I've passed through so many airports that some almost feel like my second home. Every year, I seem to travel like George Clooney's character in *Up in the Air*. One memorable booking had me flying from London to LA and New York to Rome, then back to London, and Nice to London to LA to Auckland to LA to London, then Glasgow to Copenhagen and back to London in the space of two weeks. I must have more mileage than the Exxon Valdez.

Just like restaurants, there are five-star airports and zero-star airports. Copenhagen's Kastrup airport is definitely a five, and comparing it with London's Heathrow is like comparing Cinderella with her ugliest stepsister, except for Terminal 5.

Kastrup is exquisitely designed: light, airy and spectacularly clean. You could butter bread on the pristine floors, and there's not a discarded McDonald's wrapper or beer can in sight. The furniture and check-in desks are so attractive yet functional that they wouldn't look out of place in a Philippe Starck showroom, whereas Heathrow now bears a horrid resemblance to a shopping mall. Heathrow's fast-food joints smell and its endless perfumeries and designer shops, which profess to be duty-free, give only the most minuscule of discounts (although it's not difficult to offer significant discounts off high-street prices when ours are the most overpriced in the world). Beauty products are far cheaper in the US and on the Continent, and who wants to lug Gucci bags and Burberry raincoats on to a plane? It is torturous attempting to negotiate the maze of booths, boutiques and snack bars that constitute the Heathrow infrastructure. It is, however, better than Gatwick – much as the Salem witch-burnings were a slight improvement on the Spanish Inquisition.

Nice airport has also lost the five-star status, especially where parking is concerned. It used to be so easy, but the French powers that be have fiddled with the outside of the airport to such an extent that tempers fray everywhere. In order to alleviate some of this rage and to cheer everyone up, some bright spark had come up with the misguided idea of plastering hideous posters on to almost every available surface early on during the renovation. In horrible hot colours, they were printed with a phrase containing two of the most ghastly puns I've ever seen: 'Nice To Sea You'. I've always considered the French to be the masters of culture, style and elegance, but someone should have told them that, more often than not, less is more. They recently added a rather convenient, if inappropriately titled section, considering the vast amounts of prostitutes that line the highway just outside the airport, called 'kiss 'n' fly'.

Two years ago, when I was changing planes in Mexico City (which is always a terrifying experience – someone had just been shot there the week before I arrived) the security seemed particularly over the top. 'Open it!' barked a hatchet-faced security woman pointing to my wheelie. Obediently, I opened it up and another even more officious-looking police inspector arrived and pointed to my closed tray of costume jewellery. 'Open that!' he demanded in Spanish. I requested a private room for this potentially embarrassing examination. The inspector immediately pounced upon a large fake-diamond encrusted ring – one of Kenneth Jay Lane's newest creations – and whipped out a *jeweller's magnifying glass* and proceeded to inspect it with the professionalism of Shylock. I honestly thought he was about to give me an estimate.

'It's not *real*,' Percy told him in Spanish. The cop then inspected some earrings and several bracelets with great zeal.

'We're going to miss the plane,' I whispered as the cop lovingly caressed some fake Chanel pearls.

Percy finally snapped, 'It's *all* costume jewellery.' The cop then turned to us with a faint smile and said in perfect English, 'Very nice . . . couldn't tell the difference,' as he magnanimously waved us away.

Travelling anywhere today is becoming more and more tedious, particularly the endless and intrusive security procedures. I'm often unlucky enough to be picked out for those euphemistically titled 'special searches' (due to my obvious resemblance to one of America's Most Wanted no doubt), and I try to endure them with stoic indifference as I stand there, coatless, shoeless, hatless and sunglass-less, arms akimbo like a scarecrow whilst the officer in charge wearing the grim, sadistic expression of an Alcatraz security guard runs what looks somewhat like a cattle prod far too close for comfort around my pelvis. It is not what I would call a 'good look', particularly if some sly soul having just gone through the same procedure sneaks a couple of snaps on his mobile phone, which he'll invariably email to his mates or upload to the Internet. Nevertheless, refusing to do a Naomi Campbell, I close my eyes and think of England as the contents of everything in my carry-on are minutely examined.

The Feds are also out in force at JFK airport in New York. Tough non-compromising uniformed cops now stand guard, instead of the indolent-looking amateurs we were accustomed to. Going through security these days you are greeted and searched by lynx-eyed professional men and women who wouldn't look out of place behind the barrel of a Kalashnikov. It does make one feel more secure, but it can also cause a great deal of embarrassment. I remember seeing one young man who, after beeping when going through the X-ray machine, was probed by a keen lady officer armed with her security fairy wand. His metal buckle continued to make the pesky thing bleep, but instead of asking him to remove his belt, the officer diligently ran her machine over and over the front of his skin-tight trousers until, lo and behold and to the amusement of fellow passengers, we noticed it wasn't a gun in his pocket at all!

Although I totally understand airport security must be super vigilant these days, sometimes it can nevertheless be despotically extreme, as demonstrated by a minor horror story I was told. A well-known actress was about to walk through the X-ray machine at JFK while holding her eighteen-month-old infant when a brusque security guard stopped her.

'Can he walk?' he inquired of the infant.

'He's just learning,' she replied.

'If he can walk then he's got to walk across by himself – that's the rules,' he stated with the authority of a Gestapo commandant. 'Put him down.'

'But he doesn't *like* walking,' protested the bemused mother, as the baby was wrenched from her arms and planted on its tiny feet.

Armageddon ensued. But the security guard insisted and the poor little chap started bawling his lungs out as the frantic mother was rushed through the sensor trying to encourage him to follow her, which he steadfastly refused to do. Unable to comprehend why he'd been so unceremoniously dumped on the floor, he threw himself screaming to the ground, while a gaggle of adults, including the security guards, tried to coax him through the X-ray machine. In spite of his mother's continued protestations that he was not ready for this terrifying toddler trial, the officials continued to insist upon it, and after several minutes of cajoling, the distraught child managed to cross the barrier under his own steam, at which point the buzzer went off and the sobbing child had to be thoroughly body searched because the rivets in his little jeans set the sensors off!

Now all airports are becoming even more intrusive

with the introduction of the body-scan machines. I cannot imagine a more invasive procedure than this virtual cavity search and wonder if it would perhaps be more bearable if they teamed it up with medical tests detecting cancers and polyps. (Recently a doctor refused to submit to the body scan saying that it could cause cancer. Since I travel a great deal I find this a terrifying prospect, even if the powers that be deny that these machines cause adverse reactions.) I dread to think of what would happen if some of the more high-profile scans were leaked out to the press. At LA airport, the small area where you queue to get the demeaning security search is often teeming with paparazzi. They adore the situation where stars without their shoes, jackets or headgear are frisked by security men and women. I asked the head of the LA police department if something could be done about it and he told me: 'It's a public place – it's [the photographers'] right.' What about the rights of an individual, who just happens to be a famous actor, not to be pushed and shoved and have a camera poked inches away from their face? Now outside the airport at LA the paparazzi are free to prey on hapless celebrities as if they were Romans watching the gladiators. Do people really want to see the distinguished actor, Sydney Poitier, shoeless, with his arms outstretched, being body searched?

I have always been keenly security conscious. My mother instilled in me the necessity to double-lock all doors and windows and to never trust strangers (especially men) and generally stressed that prevention is far better than a rapid response system. Those of you who know me know that I am in favour of more police on the streets and tougher measures on those who offend, even in small ways, because I am convinced that small offences lead to larger ones, and it's best to nip certain buds.

I am well aware of the potential for danger inherent in modern-day travel, and I keep a sharp eye out for anyone suspicious, either at the airport or on the plane. I always submit to the *de rigueur* security checks with impunity, glad that all my carry-on bags are being thoroughly examined, even if I have to swallow the small humiliation of having my personal belongings on display and my concern that some amateur pap could potentially use the moment to embarrass me publicly.

However, I find it a little odd that in the years of travelling since 11 September, I have *always* – not once or twice, but invariably *always* – been singled out for not only the body search at the checkpoint, but also at the gate. Percy can attest to this, and it's become a sort of joke between us. Sometimes he calls me 'my wife, the terrorist' (but never in front of the security people). He, for some reason, never gets searched.

One such memorable 'random' search I had was at the gate of a Virgin airlines flight to LA. Most of the other passengers were allowed on board, and were no doubt entertained by a close-up look at me being detained. Four security men stared grimly at me, ignoring other potential security threats. When the female security guard approached me with the intention of frisking me by hand, I politely (I thought) but firmly requested the electronic wand, which is available for exactly that purpose. Her superior, staring at me equally menacingly, refused this request and I was subjected to a hand search, which I have to say is a degrading, invasive and altogether unpleasant experience, made more so by the rowdy commentary of a couple of passing passengers.

I realize that it's politically incorrect not to do random searches, because certain racial types might feel offended, or singled out, so therefore these random searches are the 'fair' alternative – and I submit subserviently. As a high-profile, recognizable person, it may be that I am being used as an example to others.

I have noticed that in the case of men's searches not much attention is paid to their genital area (apart from the search of the unfortunate gentleman in my earlier anecdote) – the guards discreetly run their hands up to and just below the inseam of the trousers, but no further. Unfortunately not so in the case of women. Surely more could be concealed in a male pouch?

I want to feel that the security services at airports are intelligent enough to recognize major threats from minor ones, and are capable of making decisions on the spot. Yet at Heathrow, the airlines hire private companies to carry out secondary security, regulated by the government, not by the company paying for their services. Therefore, these companies have no influence on what the security teams do nor on how they do it. The cost of hiring these private security firms is passed on to the ticket buyer in order to keep the airlines flying.

Actor James Woods was on a United Airlines domestic flight three days before September 11 and saw four men behaving suspiciously. With an actor's eye, he felt they could be potential threats and reported their behaviour to the FBI. Absolutely nothing was done to investigate these men, who turned out to be four of the terrorists who brought the plane down and the world to a standstill on that fateful day. If we are indeed a world under constant threat of a terrorist attack, then our governments should stop trying to shortchange us on the security staff who are supposed to safeguard us.

Trains are hardly much better. I was looking forward to relaxing on the Eurostar from Paris to London. No airport hassle to get through or the dreaded removal of shoes (which provokes in me the fear of verrucas), belt, coat, hat and jewellery. So I was surprised when, as I casually walked through security at Gare du Nord wearing my usual gold bangles, the beeper beeped furiously. 'Get back!' barked the burly security guard as he raised his hand indicating where he wanted me, and knocking my fedora off in the process. 'Take them off!' he yelled again as I just stood, stupidly wondering what he meant – this wasn't a strip club after all. He gestured to my bracelets as if they were vipers, hissing, 'Off, off, take them off.' To say I was nonplussed at the almost Gestapo level of security was putting it mildly. I prised off my bracelets, breaking a nail in the process, and handed the offensive trinkets to another official, who seemed to be enjoying my discomfort. He examined them minutely, turning them around and inspecting them as if I had managed to secret an illegal substance inside them, destined to blow everyone on the train to kingdom come. He finally returned them with a big grin. 'Thank you very much, Ms Collins. I always enjoyed *Dynasty*.'

Every time I check in at an airport, I'm amused by those statutory questions about my luggage. Sometimes they are asked in a tone of understandably bored resignation, at other times with sparkling enthusiasm, as if the person were actually interested in your replies. It's as if some acting coach has put some of them through their paces – 'Now, my dears, think of yourselves as a particularly charismatic prosecuting counsel, determined to get at the truth. Let's try it again – big smile – eye contact – off you go. Did you pack these yourself?' This always evokes an anecdote about the late-lamented Lord Warwick. The handsome and charming 'Brookie' was checking in for a flight to Spain, when he was asked if he had packed his suitcases himself.

'Packed them *myself*?' he replied with astonishment. 'Good Lord! The very idea . . .'

As I spend a great deal of time on aeroplanes, I've often wondered what is the correct etiquette when confronted with someone sitting within ten feet of me who starts coughing or sneezing, without the benefit of so much as a used tissue to cover their mouth or nostrils. As a fully paid-up member of Hypochondriacs Anonymous, I'm immediately panic-stricken that I'm on the verge of contracting a virulent strain of antibiotic resistant tuberculosis. I bury my face in my airline pillow or a sweater until I feel the bugs have passed over me. I then usually catch the sneezer looking at me huffily as if I've done something wrong. Maybe I should always travel with my own oxygen tent, or sport a Michael Jackson-type surgical mask as the Japanese do. I have found a compromise now by applying a small amount of anti-biotic ointment in each nostril before I board the plane. Don't laugh – it works, and you won't get haemorrhoids in your nose!

The last time I experienced the true glamour of travelling was when I flew on Concorde.

Ah, Concorde – the very word conjures up style – sleek, sophisticated, yes, even sexy and . . . surreal? Hurtling through the atmosphere eleven miles above Earth at speeds that would sling your upper lip over your head was not so very long ago a flight of fancy, yet this became the routine of those fortunate enough to afford the pricetag for almost thirty years. It seems only yesterday that the world gasped anxiously when Concorde was banned from flying over land, surely driving the last nail in the coffin, only to breathe a sigh of relief when the skies over New York opened to permit the crucial London/Paris to New York route, allowing Concorde to race around the globe.

My first trip in the mid-eighties was a true white-knuckler. I had taken a flight from LA to New York, slogging and lurching through rain-soaked skies for an unusually long eight hours, in order to board the Concorde to London. When I boarded, the cramped conditions did nothing to mollify my already frazzled nerves. The sight of a supermodel *sans maquillage* snoozing contentedly in her seat opposite me made me envious of whatever drugs I supposed she was taking (she told me later that she had taken the trip dozens of times and so felt fairly *laissez faire* about the flight). I plugged my ears waiting for the loud blast I fully expected when we broke the sound barrier, the same one I had heard from Earth, and was amazed when only the most imperceptible lurch meant we had gone supersonic. Later, the captain invited me into the cockpit to view the magnificent sight of London as we circled above. It was only after my apprehension eased that I realized I had been whisked there in less than half the time it had taken me to get to New York from LA – and on the smoothest ride since Häagen Dazs. I was hooked.

Why would anyone want to travel any other way? So what if Aunt Maisie's windows get blown off just because she lives under the flight path? (Actually, they wouldn't – Concorde at top speed wouldn't stress fine crystal even three times closer to the ground.) So what if our ears are ringing until kingdom come with sonic booms to rival Gabriel's Horn? If we can get there in half the time, why wouldn't we want to? *That* was truly progress!

But it was not to be. The beautiful gas-guzzler just

took up too much of that precious resource and took far too much work to maintain. Furthermore, due to the potential damage to the environment, there weren't enough destinations for Concorde to crisscross the world and compete with subsonic airliners; thus, alas, we lay to rest the last remnant of the glorious age of supersonic commercial flights. What a tragedy.

Nevertheless, I write not to bury Concorde, no, I write to praise it. Concorde stood testament to the hope of a younger, perhaps more naive, but I think more optimistic and, to my mind, happier world. Britain, and France, should stand proud of its achievements. We should remember that fine day in 1976 when the first commercial Concorde flights departed, at the exact same time – Air France from Charles De Gaulle bound for Rio de Janeiro, British Airways from Heathrow headed for Bahrain – marking the moment when British and French technological know-how surpassed the aerospace domination heretofore allotted to the US and the Soviet Union (although, to be fair, the USSR did actually get the first supersonic passenger aircraft up, and did reach supersonic speed first). They might have been the first to put a man on the moon, but by God we were the first to make it commercially viable to whisk 100 people from their breakfast table in London to another breakfast table in New York – regularly and vice versa.

Britain and France went about the project in a true state of cooperation, for once. There may have been the odd argument, like whether Concorde should be spelled with or without an 'e', which, in true Brit fashion, was graciously unknotted by Sir Anthony Wedgwood Benn when he said, 'It means 'E'xcellence, 'E'ngland, 'E'urope and 'E'ntente!'. But on the whole there existed a true fifty-fifty partnership, burying, if at least for the sake of that project, centuries of rivalry and heralding the age of the British/French Rolls-Royce/Snecma Olympus engines that faithfully served Concorde for many years. And what about that day in 1973, when Concorde, windows rigged with telescopes, took a fleet of American, French and British scientists on a mission to chase the solar eclipse, giving them an unprecedented seventy-four minutes of viewing?

There were so many other unexpected benefits. I'm sure the statistics exist about how positive an impact Concorde had on economics and business. I can state categorically that travelling from London to New York in the same amount of time it now takes to cross that damn traffic light from the Mall into Trafalgar Square was immensely morale-boosting.

When I was invited on Concorde's bittersweet last flight from New York to London, I was as excited as a kid going to Disneyland. As Concorde was one of Britain's greatest ambassadors, I considered it too important an historic event to miss. Percy and I arrived at a darkened and seemingly deserted JFK airport at 6 a.m. for the 7 a.m. flight.

'Are we the first?' I enquired of the charming special-services representative.

'No, you're the last,' was the reply. 'The party's been going for hours.'

We checked in without luggage, which in itself is a personally historic event, but I still managed to pocket a couple of Concorde luggage tags. I understand they are now selling on eBay alongside various other mementos such as memorabilia catalogues, safety cards and a bathroom sign – God only knows how they took that off!

We made our way to the party atmosphere in the departure lounge, where luminaries and celebrities quaffed champagne and gave interviews right, left and centre to the eager American and British press. When I was interviewed, I said I thought it was tragic that this magnificent piece of cutting-edge technology was going to be phased out and that I hoped that another company, perhaps Virgin Atlantic, would keep it going as it had been rumoured. Just before embarking I popped into the loo and whilst combing my hair was asked by a nervous BA press officer if I would do her a big favour.

'But of course!' I replied graciously. 'Do you have a pen?'

'Oh, I . . . I don't want your autograph,' she said. 'But would you mind not mentioning Richard Branson any more in your articles?'

The flight was called a short time later and the entire New York-based BA staff lined up to say their goodbyes to everyone, many of them with tears in their eyes. It was still dark outside, but it seemed as though the entire airport ground staff had stopped what they were doing and stood on the tarmac to wave and cheer. On board, the champagne was poured lavishly as we privileged few buckled up and prepared for the last ride. I clutched Percy's hand as the brakes were released and the power of a sudden 250-miles-per-hour acceleration lurched us against the back of our seats, as if we were passengers on some insanely powerful hot-rod competition, but then we soared up into the air on this majestic, beautiful and graceful bird.

We were an eclectic group – there was one couple who had paid £40,000 for the privilege, several businessmen who had crossed the Atlantic at least twice a week for many years, and a few prizewinners. Back in steerage (although all seats are considered equal), sat some distinguished members of the press, along with a sprinkling of ageist left-wing hacks. The Royal Ballet's prima ballerina Darcey Bussell helped start the autograph-collecting frenzy whilst the staff did a grand job jostling with TV cameras, crew and photographers to manoeuvre the trolleys and trays down the narrow aisle. In the back, Jeremy Clarkson, in a snit, threw a glass of water all over Piers Morgan who was then the editor of the *Daily Mirror*, but overall there was so much hilarity that Piers implored us join him. We attempted to do so but there was such a crush of flight attendants, revellers and media that it was impossible.

As we approached Heathrow, the captain's announcement brought a sense of solemnity through the cabin. Everyone fixed their gaze intently out of the windows, seeing London pass underneath – cars stopped on the M4 and people waved at us from fields, while the Millennium Dome and the London Eye stood impassive in their farewell to Concorde. The flight attendants walked down the aisle, bidding Godspeed to the regular faces they had become so accustomed to seeing regularly on that NY-LON run, and thanking them for the memories shared. Everyone felt slightly choked up when we landed and saw those hundreds of thousands of people who had turned out to say goodbye to their favourite, never-to-be-replaced aeroplane. Concorde may be dead, but it will live long in memory. What a way to go.

With Concorde no longer an option, my absolute favourite method of travelling is by private plane. How luxurious, how glamorous, how effortlessly exhilarating to recline in some rich friends' soft-leather upholstery, sipping a glass of Chablis whilst a smiling flight attendant discreetly deals with your luggage. And . . . there is no beastly security and shoe removal to go through beforehand.

Most of my trips on a private plane have been superb, except for one ghastly experience. Boarding a friend's plane in LA to go to New York, I was ushered into the master stateroom complete with a huge double bed, suede-covered walls, a plasma-screen TV and every other modern convenience imaginable.

I called my friend Judy to boast about this scrumptious opulence as we started to ascend over the Pacific Ocean.

While I was looking out of the window I saw a strange yellow liquid pouring from the back of the plane. I laughingly said to Judy, 'I wonder what it is?' Just then there was a sharp tap at the door. A nervous flight attendant said, 'I'm sorry Ms Collins, but we have a slight engine problem so we are dumping fuel for half an hour and then heading back to LA.'

'WHAAAT?!' I yelled. 'It's not possible. Mr X said he's never had any problem with this plane.'

'Sorry,' she replied. 'Please fasten your seat belt, it could get bumpy.'

Well that was it for the gorgeous private 747. I had to wait instead at LA airport for six hours before finally boarding a tiny puddle jumper to New York. Not the same at all.

On Men: Can't Live with 'Em, Can't Kill 'Em . . .

'Men! Rough hairy beasts!' exclaims Jack Lemmon in *Some Like it Hot*. That was fifty years ago and now they seem rougher, hairier and beastlier than ever. When we threw manners out the window, we also threw out the code of chivalry and ethics that men used to adhere and aspire to. What we are left with now are the bland metrosexuals or the Neanderthal lumps.

I like men – that should be fairly obvious – and I admit there may be one or two good ones around, but it seems to me that so many of the perfect gentlemen bat for the other side (and I can hardly blame them considering how unfeminine many women have become), leaving today's girls with few choices.

I despair for my two daughters' futures as regards to men and lasting relationships. All the good men are married, or too young, or if they haven't been married by the time they're thirty-five well, there must be something wrong with them.

Further complicating lasting relationships is the changing concept of commitment. Long-term relationships seem no longer fashionable, and couples break up at the mere hint of a rift. Erstwhile one took the step of marriage with care because it was meant to be a lifelong union and couples found ways to cope when things were bumpy. As time passed two people who stayed together found a balance, so that companionship and partnership was nurtured. I unfortunately was part of the generation that began to view (and sometimes welcome) divorce as an acceptable alternative. We were fed up with the patronizing options our mothers had put up with – abusive, belittling or cheating men and men who treated them like Stepford wives. But a side-effect of our willingness to divorce was that we lost the concept of fighting to stay together.

As an incurable romantic, I still believe that marriage and commitment are high on the list of the most import-ant things in life, which is why in my ten-year marriage to Percy we have been absolutely certain of our lifelong commitment to each other.

On Men

I believe most women are deep down also romantics. Somewhere buried in our DNA, whether it's because of the fairy-tale-princess-and-knight-in-shining-armour stories we are brought up on or whether it's our pre-programmed gift as the only sex capable of nurturing a child in our wombs and giving birth, it is natural for us to seek and try to choose a mate for life. Unfortunately, many men don't seem to be on our emotional wavelength and shy away from marriage. There is a saying: 'Why buy the cake when you can have a slice for free?' and I think that most men can't be bothered to go that step further if they're already sleeping with their girlfriends. Perhaps I have been a part of this change of sentiment, because I consider myself to be an emancipated woman having lived with a few men without marrying them (shock horror!).

One of the delicious advantages of living in LA is the plethora of wonderful classic movies from the thirties to the fifties that are constantly aired on all the cable channels in the afternoons or in the very early mornings. Looking at those men on screen is an eye-opener. What strikes me most is how hunky and masculine the majority of the male stars were.

Boom Town featured two extremely macho co-stars: Spencer Tracy and Clark Gable. Although Gable was by far the better looking and taller (he kept referring to Tracy as 'Shorty' in the film) Spencer Tracy was his equal in the he-man department. He was just such a good actor, and had enormous charisma and buckets of charm.

Most of the male stars from the golden era of Hollywood were macho: Anthony Quinn dancing the tango with Rita Hayworth in *Blood And Sand* oozed masculine sex appeal, as did his co-star Tyrone Power; John Garfield in *The Postman Always Rings Twice*, with gorgeous Lana Turner, sizzled a great deal more than the pale remake with Jessica Lange and Jack Nicholson.

Garfield was a true man's man and somewhat of a ladies' man, too. He died in bed with his mistress, 'on the job' as they say. In contrast to these wonderful men, many of today's modern actors look a bit wimpy to me.

Scientists have come to an unusual conclusion about the phenomenon of today's 'pretty-boy' actors compared with the he-men of yesteryear. It seems that as the nation's health improves, women's tastes in the men they fancy softens. When health is poor and times are tough, women go for rugged, tough-looking types, who they expect will give them strong babies. Hence, during the Depression and the war, they flocked to see Douglas Fairbanks, Victor Mature, Humphrey Bogart, Burt Lancaster, Kirk Douglas and Mr Über-Macho, John Wayne.

But when a nation's health improves, and life-expectancy rises, women become attracted to more feminine-looking men, who appear to have gentler natures.

One poll that interviewed 5,000 women had Zac Efron beat Sean Connery by a long shot. Today's women it seems prefer more cutesy-looking movie stars such as Robert Pattinson and Taylor Lautner, stars of those *Twilight* vampire movies, and now seventeen-year-old

Justin Bieber, all of whom are mobbed whenever they appear in public.

But as a young girl, that wasn't the kind of man I went for. I wrote to many of the post-war British 'Idols of the Odeons' for autographed photos and most of those I wrote to were tall, dark and broodingly handsome.

When these photographs came back, they were proudly stuck under my school-desk lid. I had James Mason, Stewart Granger and Maxwell Reed; in fact, so taken was I by the latter that I foolishly married him when I was eighteen – what a mistake!

Maxwell was fourteen years my senior and ten inches taller than me. My idiotic reasons for marrying him were that not only had he been my favourite movie star whilst I was at school but also that he'd taken my virginity. 'Taken' was the operative word – Maxwell date raped me on our first date, and I felt so guilty I agreed to marry him some months later.

The marriage was a fiasco from the get-go. I even knew it on the night before the wedding when I cried buckets and begged my parents to call it off. Tall, dark and handsome he was but the jet-black hair turned out to be a dye job and in the first month of our marriage I actually was commanded to lean over the sink to apply the black goop to his hair and eyebrows!

He wore lifts so he wasn't as tall as he looked on screen. His curly hair was permed and his dark eyes heavily mascaraed and, as I found out on the honeymoon, he was an abusive bully who couldn't bear another man to talk to his young bride. I even had to watch him parading nude in front of the house detectives at our hotel room when we interrupted a burglary! He had some dodgy connections with the underworld too and often threatened me, saying, 'I'll cut up your pretty little face if you even think of leaving me.' In the folly and ignorance of my youth I put up with everything, including his uninspired performance between the sheets.

'My Mama done tol' me' that 'men only want one thing' and that 'it's not very nice but just close your eyes and think of something else'. How innocent most young girls were in the fifties beggars belief! We had no sex education and were supposed to be little more than chattels, *hausfraus* and obedient to our husbands. When I told a British tabloid that 'I shall do no cooking or cleaning in my marriage' I was severely castigated for not being a real woman! Since I was an actress under contract to Rank, rising at dawn and returning from work late at night, I felt I was within my rights not to fit the requisite slot for how a supposedly 'real woman' should behave.

I stood for it for as long as I could, (luckily escaping frequently on theatrical tours and film locations) because I knew the shame I would bring to my parents if I left him.

The final crunch came one frosty night at Les Ambassadeurs nightclub. A lecherous-looking Arab man at the next table had been staring down my dress all night, and when I returned from the ladies room Max was deep in conversation with him. He turned and whispered to me eagerly, 'He wants to spend the night with you! He will pay us £10,000! And I can even watch!'

I was so shocked I couldn't even argue as he went on bleating about how we could buy a cottage and go to Hollywood and become stars. But that was it for me. I burst into tears and ran home to the sanctity of my parents' flat. Luckily, a short time later I was signed for a fabulous part in *Land of the Pharaohs*, which was shooting in Rome.

But woe was me – Mr Reed also landed a movie job there. He had recently been photographed for a tabloid holding up a picture of me and whining to the reporter along the lines of 'she has everything now. I'm broke and on the way down. I made her a star and she won't give me anything. She should pay me support', and so forth. How pathetic is that? Shades of *A Star is Born* – but I ignored it.

One day, whilst sunbathing on the beach with my mother and young brother at Fregene, outside Rome, Max appeared, looming over me, demanding I return all the jewellery and money he'd given me. We were still married, although separated, and I was not earning very much – £50 a week at Rank and somewhat more for *Pharaohs*. He insisted I give him everything in my savings account, 'otherwise the boys will get you'. My mother was outraged and gave him a piece of her mind but he ignored her and stalked off, looking ridiculous in too-tight shorts. But I was so terrified, I sent a few trinkets to his hotel – a couple of rings (he even wanted the wedding ring back) and a charm bracelet and necklace, which was all the jewellery I possessed.

I had to wait three years for a divorce and by the time proceedings came to court I was in Hollywood. One day, whilst shooting a bathtub scene and covered in suds for *The Opposite Sex*, a server slapped me with a subpoena to appear in court in Santa Monica and give Maxwell Reed the money he 'deserved'.

My lawyer advised that, since I was now earning the princely sum of $1,250 a week, which would rise in five years to $5,000 a week, I should pay up or Reed could drag the case on for years and eventually be granted more. 'He said he discovered you,' said my lawyer.

'But that's a lie!' I said furiously. The threats of carving my face up also made me break out in nightmare sweats.

So I went to court with my sister Jackie and the divorce cost me over $10,000. Since I didn't have it, I had to borrow from the studio and I had to pay Max's and my own legal fees and give him all the money in my bank account – about $1,500! I know this doesn't sound like much today but in 1958 it was a fortune. The judge cross-examined me curiously as to why I had to pay a forty-year-old man so much, but I was so desperate to get rid of him that I persuaded him and he reluctantly granted me the divorce.

And that was divorce number one!

Soon after arriving in Hollywood I went to the party of a

millionaire playboy and met three of the most stunning actors of the twentieth century: Marlon Brando, James Dean and Paul Newman. All blue jeaned and beer sipping, they were sitting together on a sofa, chilling out with each other.

Although Marlon was the sexiest and Jimmy the moodiest, far and away the handsomest and most charismatic was 'PL' as his friends called him. Paul was almost too beautiful, but his crooked nose and jutting chin tempered the look and made him a true hunk, and those eyes were indeed icy-blue.

I believe that Paul embodied what I consider a real man to be – one with uncomplicated goals and simple choices but never ungallant or brutish. He loved his wife dearly, they had a long-lasting and successful marriage, and he had a sincere and deep belief in giving to others without being a sanctimonious 'look at what a great guy I am' prig.

Paul had a fabulous sense of humour and loved cooking, and drinking his beer straight from the bottle. I asked him if he ever got a hangover from all that beer and he told me his recipe for curing a hangover was a cold shower, followed by a hot one and then another cold one, and finally 'dipping my face in a tub of ice for five minutes – you gotta try it'. Well, I did try the ice bit once and it was totally horrible and made my face bright red all day long. However, I had to laugh when that memorable scene in *The Sting* featured his secret recipe. And it worked for him, because he never looked as if he'd had more than a sip of booze. He was extremely disciplined and he did hundreds of push-ups and sit-ups daily – the reason why he kept that trim physique all his life. He was quite macho, but in a laid back, non-aggressive way.

That was a time when young actors were attempting to break away from the square-jawed heroic leading man image personified by Gregory Peck, Cary Grant and Alan Ladd. This new breed of actors were aiming to be perceived as dangerous and different. Paul, Marlon, Jimmy Dean, Montgomery Clift and Steve McQueen all played troubled and flawed anti-heroes, and they raised the bar as to what a leading man should be.

When Joanne Woodward won her Oscar for *The Three Faces of Eve* I went to the ceremony with her and Paul. We were so excited as she went up to the stage to receive her award. Although Joanne hadn't really expected to win, PL had been encouraging her in his charming jokey fashion during the nail-biting week that led to the event. She had made her own green taffeta dress by hand – and Paul wouldn't stop telling her how beautiful she looked and complimenting her that she was one of a kind, a great beauty and a great talent. He absolutely adored his wife and I believe was totally faithful to her in the many years of their marriage. This was despite the fact that many starlets (and some stars) threw their caps at him. But he was so down-to-earth that he never fell for the adulation.

He used to joke at parties about *The Silver Chalice*, one of those awful pseudo-religious movies Hollywood churned out. 'It was the worst movie I ever made,' he would sigh whilst cradling one of his many beers. 'I wore a white-silk Greek cocktail dress – I looked like a freak!'

20th Century Fox, the studio I was under contract to, cast the Newmans in *Rally Round the Flag, Boys*, a comedy about the shenanigans surrounding the building of a space station in a small town. The studio insisted that Jayne Mansfield, their current sex symbol, play the role of witty, vampy Angela, who uses all her wiles to seduce Harry, played by Paul. But since the Newmans and I were good friends, they lobbied the studio head to get me the role. He replied, 'Brunettes aren't funny – blondes are funny. Joan can't play comedy.'

'She can! She can be hilarious!' Newman insisted, and he continued to insist until finally the studio caved in. I was delighted to be playing opposite Paul and alongside Joanne and we had tons of fun on the set. In one scene Paul and I had to get fiercely and hilariously drunk (something of which we both had experience) in my character's apartment. We danced a mad cha-cha, bumping derrieres and screeching with laughter, I then chased him around and finally got him onto the sofa and he lay back with a beatific smile on his face whilst I stroked the back of his neck with my foot! Then we fell about giggling madly onto the floor when suddenly he leapt up, grabbed the chandelier and started swinging all over the set. The scene was so long it took all day to shoot, and as the day progressed Paul and I got more Method-actor-like and both of us actually started feeling quite drunk even though we hadn't touched a drop. We spouted out our lines, rather convincingly we both thought, amidst screams of laughter throughout. But our old director Leo McCarey did not agree. As Paul swung on the chandelier like a handsome gorilla the director yelled, 'Cut! Will ya stop all this laughing crap? We're making a comedy here, for Chrissakes!'

This only caused us to laugh even harder, particularly since the crew was trying to suppress giggles themselves. We felt like a rabble of naughty children in church with Leo McCarey playing the stern rector. In the last part of the scene Paul crawls to the front door to escape Angela's clutches. I tripped and my bottom ended up next to his face, at which he quipped, 'Angela Hoffa – I'd know that face anywhere!' The laughter dam burst and luckily it was the last shot that day because nothing else could have been done with a straight face after that.

In 1963, my second husband Tony Newley and I rented the Newmans' cosy Fifth Avenue apartment to stay in whilst I was expecting my first baby. We visited the Newmans' wonderful farmhouse in Connecticut on many weekends. Every night Paul would barbecue, making excellent burgers with secret ingredients he refused to divulge. He also made the most delicious salad dressings. A few years later, as we all know, he started selling these dressings as 'Newman's Own' with all proceeds going to charity. He was extremely concerned about under-privileged and seriously ill children and started his Hole in the Wall Gang chain of summer camps for kids at a time when charitable institutions were rather scarce and ones helmed by a single figurehead were non-existent.

The last time I saw Paul was in 2007 at a New York charity event for the Christopher Reeve foundation, which raised money for stem-cell research and for which Paul was a strong advocate. I thought he looked thin but still extremely handsome. The self-deprecating charm flowed from him as we hugged, kissed and reminisced.

'You're looking good, Collins,' he flirted.

'So are you, PL,' I flirted back.

'I still gotta pulse,' he grinned, those famous eyes twinkling.

Once at a party we played a morbid game where we all suggested our own epitaphs. Beer in hand as always, Paul quipped, 'Here lies Paul Newman, who died a failure because his eyes turned brown!'

He was one of a kind.

I was lucky enough to appear in a series of films with many attractive and masculine-looking male stars in Hollywood: Gregory Peck in *The Bravados* was not only extremely handsome and a great actor, but he was also one of the most elegant and gentlemanly of all, without ever losing his masculine appeal or his tough side.

In contrast to Gregory Peck's chivalry, though, was the Neanderthal-like Richard Burton, whom I played opposite in *Sea Wife*. He immediately made no secret of the fact that he was not only the ultimate seducer, but the leader of the pack of hell-raisers. He made the obligatory pass that all actors did then and charmingly admitted to me that he would 'f*** a snake if it were wearing a skirt!' He also told me that if I did not succumb to his charms, I would ruin his record of sleeping with all his leading ladies. He was one of that rare breed – a truly macho movie star who expected all women to succumb. But in no way was I tempted, although I saw other women fall like ninepins at his feet, Elizabeth Taylor being no exception on *Cleopatra*.

Other hell-raisers and drinking buddies of Burton were Oliver Reed, Richard Harris and Peter O'Toole. All of them good examples of the macho heterosexual movie stars of the sixties and seventies.

I worked with Richard Harris in *Game for Vultures*, shot in South Africa. It was a pretty boring shoot, so a lot of drinking took place – on and off the set. I must admit I was involved in a few marathon boozing sessions with Richard, but even after a night of debauchery we both always knew our lines the next day. It would have been bad manners not to – and I'm not sure the same could be said of today's hell-raisers . . .

I never worked with Peter O'Toole but I once sat next to him on a Los Angeles to New York flight. He dared me to match him drink for drink so I tried. He won, and the seven-hour flight was lost in a blur of vodka martinis. Silly me.

When I worked with the fabulous Robert Mitchum in *The Big Sleep* I was quite nervous because of his tough-guy reputation, and I expected to be black and blue from the fight scene we had scheduled. I'd just finished a film with another hard man – Jack Palance – who'd roughed me up severely in our fight scene. He was a bully and pushed me around savagely, no doubt to prove how butch he was, and left my arms bruised.

But Mitchum, who epitomized the strong, silent type, was as gentle with me as if he were playing with a kitten. He had to wrestle me to the floor, fling me across the room, grab my hair, twist my neck and then, for the grand finale, throw me across his knee and spank me!

Well, I hardly felt a thing throughout, and when I asked him how he had managed to make the fight so realistic without leaving the tiniest mark on me, he replied in his laconic manner: 'Honey, it's called acting. I've been doin' this for about a hundred years – I'm an actor who knows how to play rough, and I'm not about to hurt an actress just for a goddamn scene.'

Another manly star of that era also joined us on *Dynasty* for one episode. When Charlton Heston walked on to the set, everyone practically genuflected. One of the handful of great leading men of the fifties and sixties, he received the respect he deserved, and he carried with him the most enormous directors' chair I'd ever seen!

Many of these actors, as macho and manly as they were, also had an aura of 'don't mess with me, kiddo'. I met Humphrey Bogart at a party soon after my arrival in Hollywood and because of his reputation for being nasty (just like his movie characters!) he scared me to death. I'd said something silly about another actress at a party in front of him and Frank Sinatra, and to teach me a lesson he pulled my off-the-shoulder blouse out and snapped it back, causing me great embarrassment. However, as I got to know him better I learned he was a simple family man without pretensions or delusions.

Today's slightly metrosexual-looking actors don't compare with the stars of yesteryear. Johnny Depp, Leonardo DiCaprio and Jude Law are all wonderful actors, but they are chameleon-like when it comes to their place on the masculinity meter. As for the exceptions, well, there's George Clooney, and then there's George Clooney and, oh, yes, don't forget George Clooney. But I'm afraid that's about it on the macho front, although Bradley Cooper in *The Hangover* movies and Robert Downey Jr are also great.

As for most of today's TV stars, they seem just like ordinary men cut from the same mould, except possibly for Jon Hamm of *Mad Men*, who's on his way to film stardom.

I think the sexiest, most masculine male star of all time has to be Marlon Brando. In a series of spectacular performances, he put his indelible mark on what defines masculinity. Unforgettable in a dirty white T-shirt in *A Streetcar Named Desire*, wearing a beat-up old jacket in *On the Waterfront* and clad in leather motorcycle gear in *The Wild Ones*, his image will always be the most iconic and imitated.

As I've said before, I've always considered myself to be an early model of an emancipated woman so after my divorce from Maxwell I lived with several men. Although some people considered it shocking at the time it seemed pretty sensible for me to share a pad if you were in a serious relationship. So in my twenties I had a series of monogamous relationships. Sydney Chaplin, son of Charlie, was fun-loving and a million laughs when we were out but eventually I realized he preferred golf and TV to me. Then I was with Arthur Loew, Jr, the very rich scion of the MGM clan, at whose house I met Brando and Newman. Loew was the definitive playboy, loads of fun but a bit of a chauvinist, often referring to me as 'The Little Woman' or 'The Actress'.

It was at about this time that I became seriously involved with a married man. His name was George Englund and I can tell you from experience that I do not advise any young girl to have an affair with a married man, ever. However many times he tells you he loves you and will leave his wife and kids for you, he *won't*. This was a year of total misery: of waiting for him to turn up for dinner and he didn't; of hoping the phone would ring and it wouldn't. I tried to leave him several times but he was extremely charming and sophisticated and, at eight years my senior, much more worldly.

Marlon Brando was his best friend and some of the most fascinating evenings of my life were spent in my LA apartment while Marlon played his bongos and we ate ice cream from the carton, as he and George swapped anecdotes and joked with each other. They were similar in outlook and temperament and personality. No wonder I was smitten.

One dreadful afternoon when George was in my apartment his wife, actress Cloris Leachman, arrived and started banging on the door and screaming that she knew he was there with me. We were both transfixed – 'Tell her I'm not here!' hissed the coward.

I went hesitantly to the door and said 'George isn't here, Cloris'.

'I *know* he's in there, you bitch!' she screamed. 'He's my husband! Let me in!'

'I'm not dressed, Cloris. Go away!' I quickly checked that the door was locked and George came to listen while she carried on yelling and banging. After she left I told George, 'I can't go on like this – I won't. I'm twenty-five now and I want a life.'

'I'll divorce her, I promise,' he said for the umpteenth time, but of course he didn't and our affair dragged on.

Oh, beware the married man who is full of promises and whispers sweet nothings, for they are delivered with a forked tongue. It's a no-win situation and I vowed I would never become involved with one again and I never did. Unfortunately since there is such a lack of good-looking, clever, available men, too many girls still fall for the empty promises of these married guys.

During this time I went to Japan to make *Stopover Tokyo* with Robert Wagner. The way the American crew members behaved towards the Geishas in the bars and restaurants was an eye opener. Most of the men were over fifty, overweight and married but they behaved like moonstruck sophomores before these gorgeous girls. I often went out with a group of the guys and saw how the Japanese women acted with the men – fawning over them adoringly and waiting on them hand and foot. The girls behaved the same with the Japanese men, who frequented the Geisha houses every night but forbade the wives (whom they treated like chattels) to join them. Double standards? You bet!

'You Western gals should take a few lessons from these lovely ladies,' an overweight crew member informed me, as he swilled his beer and cuddled a Geisha on his fat lap. 'They're really feminine and know how to treat a guy,' he said, looking disdainfully at my jeans and T-shirt, 'and they know how to dress, too.'

I felt affronted at this moron telling me how to dress and behave with men. I thought *he* could take some lessons on how to treat a woman before he started spouting on about how we women should treat men.

Although women's lib was not yet in full flower I considered myself to be a free and emancipated woman who did not owe anything to a man. I made my own money, and lived by my own rules. But it was still considered shocking to many people then that I believed in 'free love', certainly when one wasn't in a committed relationship.

The sixties were a couple of years away and the hippie generation had not yet arrived so I was thought of as 'fast' and a 'light woman' and 'no better than she should be' for having taken several lovers without matrimony. You see, I never really just dated; I either lived with them or married them.

When Warren Beatty came into my life I embarked on another sequentially monogamous relationship for eighteen months. Warren was young and unknown initially but he soon started climbing fame's ladder, helped no doubt by the number of influential industry figures he met through me. When he proposed marriage I accepted, but we were both wary of taking such a step, so got engaged for a year. Then when I became pregnant we both made the decision that I would terminate as we weren't ready to marry just yet. In 1960, for a young actress to have a child out of wedlock was career suicide. Although Warren and I continued living together, we both started to tire of each other and eventually decided to break up.

I then went to Britain for the filming of *The Road to Hong Kong* and started dating Robert Wagner who was and still is a gentleman and a good friend. We'd worked together in Tokyo, when he was a perfect gent, and didn't cavort with the Geishas like the other crew members. RJ, as everyone calls him, took me to see the musical *Stop the World – I Want to Get Off* and when we went backstage I met Anthony Newley. Tony became my second husband and we had two wonderful children. I married Tony because at twenty-seven I was feeling broody and wanted kids. I thought he was super talented and would make a good father even though he had warned me he didn't think he could be faithful. How silly I was to ignore his warnings!

During the eighth year of our marriage Tony produced and starred in a semi-autobiographical movie called *Can*

Hieronymous Merkin Ever Forget Mercy Humppe and Find True Happiness? I played his wife in the film, called Polyester Poontang, who tries to ensnare him with their two children while he escapes and makes love to dozens of women. How closely this mirrored our lives was too much for me. I couldn't and wouldn't stand for it and at thirty-five, considering myself to be in my prime, I took the children and went back to London.

And that was divorce number two!

After Tony and I divorced he became very bitter towards me, which was deeply hurtful and very hard on the children. He insulted me in his nightclub act and in the press and I lost a great deal of respect for him. Luckily towards the end of his life we made up but I find it terrible that a man who fathered children with a woman would bad-mouth her so horribly.

So what of today's male stars? Who will top the list of my kind of hero in decades to come? Apart from Mr Clooney of course?

As much as the Brad Pitts and Daniel Craigs of this world give a physical mould and represent that mythical manly code of behaviour that most women like, the fact is that the reality falls short. It should. No one can tick all the boxes that our flights of fancy in films and books can create. Rita Hayworth used to say, 'My husbands go to bed with Gilda and wake up with me.' So our sights are naturally lowered to fit reality, rather than the illusion.

*

After my first marriage to Maxwell Reed ended I was poorer, wiser and had a distrust of men. My next two marriages were relatively happy at first and gave me three wonderful children but then I made the second biggest mistake of my life.

Peter Holm was a fading pop singer, good looking but so boring that Michael Caine referred to him as 'the Swedish comedian'. I married him at the height of my *Dynasty* fame and fortune. It was incredibly stupid of me, particularly since all my family and friends loathed him. But somehow he persuaded me to marry him, because he seemed a clever, take-charge kind of guy when I met him. He rightly told me I wasn't receiving enough money for *Dynasty* as by then I was one of the most popular female TV stars in the world. He made me fire my agents and business managers and, on this new invention the computer, he showed me how much he was making for me without 'The Bloodsuckers' as he called them. At the same time I was at the studio twelve hours a day, he was having affairs with various females.

At weekends I would have to do publicity or fittings for the dozens of outfits needed on the show, so knew nothing of this. Then he forced me to renegotiate a new contract with the *Dynasty* producers, partially by refusing to go to work. This was totally alien to my professional ethics but his ensuing horrific red-faced threats and rows and tantrums made me reluctantly go along with his plans.

I asked for a divorce shortly after our wedding and he sneered, rightly I suppose, 'You'll be a laughing stock –

divorcing after less than a year and your fourth marriage at that. People will think you're mad.' Well, I think they already thought I was. One day I started having heart palpitations and was rushed to hospital. I was put on a heart monitor by my doctor which I had to wear all the time. As soon as I got home, Peter pulled off the monitor and threw it away saying, 'It's crap. You don't need it; you're fine.' I finally went, secretly, to the best divorce lawyer in LA – Marvin Mitchelson – to end this farce.

Peter had threatened to ruin me and that if I left him he would sell stories to the tabloids about our marriage. 'I'll make them up, and they'll believe me, because you *are* Alexis,' he laughed. He was painting me as a venal vixen when in actual fact I was an exhausted, burnt-out wreck. My lawyer took control of all my papers by getting a court order and changed the locks on my new house at Cabrillo Drive so I could be allowed (yes, allowed!) to live in it safely. Holm was told to live at my old one on Bowmont Drive, which I had owned for fifteen years. The LAPD even came to make sure the rules were followed.

I held a celebratory divorce party for which David Niven, Jr brought a selection of T-shirts made up with various slogans: '*Holm*-less', 'There's no place like *Holm*', 'US Savings & *Holms*' and other choice epithets.

Then the Swede really lost it. He refused to leave my Bowmont house, even after the court had ordered him to, and he gave interviews to the press while lolling on a lilo in the swimming pool wearing only a leopard-print Speedo! He paraded and picketed outside both houses with placards stating, 'Joan, you have our $2.5M house, a home which we bought during our marriage and I am now homeless – help!' A friend of his held up another that said, 'Joan, you earn $100,000 a week because of Peter – please give him a decent home!'

It was unbelievably embarrassing – and the cheek of it! He had paid himself about half a million dollars out of my earnings and had lived rent-and-expense free off me but he couldn't afford to even rent a house?

When the divorce finally came to trial the judge was shocked by the Swede's greed. Because we had thankfully signed a pre-nuptial agreement, the judge actually ruled that since he'd taken so much during our marriage I only had to give him the nominal sum of $80,000, which I was only too happy to do. The marriage had already cost me enough both financially and emotionally and I was thrilled to get back to my life again.

And that was divorce number four!

The other side of the coin from money-grabbing men like the Swede is the one breed of male I have always done my best to stay away from at all costs: über-rich men.

'I'd rather be a rich man's darling than a poor man's slave' goes the old vaudeville ditty. Well that's certainly not the way I feel. I have never met a rich man yet who wasn't in some way flawed. Selfish and arrogant towards his woman, or women, too many of them feel the need to conquer and subdue and once they have succeeded they are too often contemptuous of their conquests.

On Men

When I first arrived in Hollywood the jungle drums of the rich-boy set quickly started beating, and the news spread that there was new young catnip in town. Within the week my telephone rang with invitations to dinners, parties and the races from several of the most eligible rich young bachelors in Beverly Hills. Well, they were considered eligible by the Hollywood 'hoi polloi' but most, I found out after I dated a few, were spoiled, egotistical and unbelievably chauvinistic.

In that long ago Golden Age in Hollywood, the dating game was just that. With the average man you went out to dinner, dancing or a film, enjoyed yourself, or not. If you did, you might try again. If you didn't, you told your answering service – then manned by actual people – to say you were out. But the rich men of BH expected more than a chaste peck on the cheek at the end of the evening. One callow billionaire once actually spouted out that horrible old chauvinistic line after I'd refused him, 'You must be frigid.' I answered with one of my favourite Oscar Wilde quotations, 'And you, sir, are a man who knows the price of everything, and the value of nothing.'

Of course I wasn't as aware then as I am now of how highly beauty *and* youth are prized in Hollywood. Men of excessive wealth view beautiful young women as objects to be bought. Once, a handsome swarthy man who looked vaguely familiar stalked me in a toyshop. When I returned home, the shop assistant called and told me, 'Aly Khan gave me $100 for your telephone number, but I refused.'

So many women have been badly burned by becoming

involved with these über-rich men: when actress Ellen Barkin divorced Ron Perlman, one of the world's richest men days before her pre-nup expired, she received a mere $20 million as opposed to a significant share of his multi-billion-dollar estate if she had managed to hold on for a few more weeks. She described her husband as a 'totally controlling man who wouldn't allow [her] to make movies' and herself as 'a good pet, but not a bimbo.'

After the divorce, when Perlman tried to approach Barkin in a restaurant, she was reported to have said, 'Don't come near me' and threw a glass of water at him.

The meanness of some rich men is, of course, legendary. A respected interior decorator friend of mine spent two years working on a mansion for a multi-billionaire Indian businessman. He had agreed to pay all the expenses but when the house was finished he bilked her out of £100,000 because 'he didn't like the marble in the bathrooms'. He refused to pay, and hired a battery of high-priced lawyers to fight her claim, which cost him far more than the money he owed her.

Another friend of mine in her late thirties is going through a horrific pre-divorce from her rich seventy-year-old husband. He wants total custody of their two-year-old child and vows not to pay her a penny. Since this is occurring in a US state than doesn't recognize the more equitable division found elsewhere, she has a nasty battle in front of her. That the courts would award a seventy-year-old man full custody of a toddler over the mother boggles the mind.

There are too many examples of women being treated like chattels by rich men, and there are so many ex-trophy wives. Beautiful and young, they marry a rich and powerful man and for several years they have everything they dreamed about. Then comes the divorce, according to what suits him, and she becomes just another ex-wife losing her looks, influence and money. Take Kelsey Grammer, who divorced his third wife to marry wife number four, who looks almost the same as number three, except younger.

It's true – I've been known to be quite snippy with these kinds of rich men. When dancing with the young millionaire Arthur Loew, Jr at a Hollywood party, my mind was elsewhere and I wasn't hanging onto his every word. He suddenly snapped, 'You are a f****** bore.' To which I replied demurely, 'And you are a boring f***'. which actually holds true for many rich men, so I've heard.

I have been caught in the 'gimme the money' trap with ex-husbands and boyfriends more times than I care to remember. These men were pathetic gold diggers, who completely let me down. I was brought up to believe that men should take care of their women, although those ideals are perceived to be quite old-fashioned by the standards of today. The fact is that now countless married and cohabitating women make more money than their partners and are more successful, but most manage to make marriage work.

For example, Guy Ritchie, eschewing Madonna's fortune and instead wanting only as much time with his sons as possible, has become a total hero to many of my female friends, who have been heaping praise upon his gentlemanly attitude: 'He'll have women lining up outside his front door'; 'He's the coolest, so down to earth'; 'There are so few real men like him nowadays' they coo.

I am so lucky to be married to Percy Gibson, a man who also has all these qualities. He is kind, thoughtful, gallant and truly cares about me and my family. I kissed a lot of frogs before I found my prince.

But do have patience. For those women who are looking for a life partner, that old saying that men are like buses and 'if you wait long enough the right one will come along' is true for a reason. I met Percy when I was in my sixties and had given up on any thoughts of marriage again. He's my soulmate and the best man I've ever known.

And that's marriage number five and for ever!

and vulgarity as our national emblem. Gone is the gentleman, welcome the absent father; gone is the English cut, welcome the builder's crack; gone is the dandy, welcome the football hooligan.

Royal Ascot, which used to be the highlight of the racing season for ladies and gentleman, has recently degenerated into a mass of badly dressed, badly behaved yobs and boors. Some of whom lie down fully clothed on the grass in full view of the Queen, and parade around fearlessly, exposing tattooed or 'fake-baked' bodies, with far too much flesh on show. Ascot's protocol was severely flouted this year when brawls started within a drunken group in one of the champagne bars.

At Aintree and Cheltenham behaviour has always been more louche but Ascot used to be the pinnacle of prestigious English racing events, where everyone behaved beautifully and dressed flawlessly. Alas, no more and I for one don't fancy going there any more.

Brits are quickly rivalling Americans as being the fattest in the world. We may also beat them in the most hideously dressed stakes too. It's no one's fault to be born ugly, but honestly, must it be worn as a symbol of pride? Is the answer to a plain face to put on 40 pounds, staple metal works to every available lobe and tattoo oneself like an Apache on the war-trail? The strident, guttural speech, the inflections garbled to virtually resemble grunts and bellows from Viking hordes, are impossible to ignore, except to their children of course who are much more energetically dispensing the chaos their parents no longer have the energy to perpetrate. Their facial expressions, their gait, their laughter, their very gestures are crude. Nowhere is this better epitomized than in the hilarious sitcom *Benidorm*.

Vulgarity has its place as a counterweight to pretension of course, but as a ruling national characteristic it is charmless, stupid and without virtue. In our desire to be egalitarian, and since it is easier to level downwards than to have aspirations of upward mobility, many middle class people have embraced and promoted the vulgarity that they wrongly assume is the characteristic of the proletariat. The problem with this is that it ceases to be just a pose and becomes what it is now: the portrait of our national character.

Of course the phenomenon of this annihilation of decent behaviour is somewhat global. Strolling around the bucolic Place des Lices in Saint Tropez – a quaint square that thanks to the French nationalistic pride has remained unchanged for centuries – you take your life in your hands on market day. Thousands of massive tourists – countless nationalities, their *avoirdupois* spilling out of their too-tight T-shirts and baggy shorts – saunter around as if they were the only humans on Earth, shoving any reasonably sized people like me aside with the fierceness of an American football player heading for a touchdown. It seems the bigger and taller people are, the less they acknowledge the existence of others, and often force you off the pavement into the oncoming traffic with singular disregard for your safety.

Even worse, many of them have this mania for lugging what looks like their entire worldly possessions in giant rucksacks on their backs like refugees from some cataclysmic disaster. What could they possibly be packing in there? Supplies for a long trip in the Tundra? What makes these 'camel people', as I've coined them, a menace to decent folk is that they are completely unaware of this extra girth attached to their already gargantuan shoulders. They whirl around suddenly with no regard for the hapless people around them, who are then forced to dodge and sidestep to avoid serious bodily harm as you risk being crushed by some colossal ogre.

Today's Neanderthal-type males are shaped totally differently to the way men looked just a few decades ago, and with their increased girth and height seems to come increased rudeness. They push you out of the way, blow cigarette smoke in your face and use profanity freely. But it's not only the males of the species. The females can be equally, if not more, spiteful and self-centred.

I observed one lady's coarse behaviour recently when I went grocery shopping at the giant *Geant* hypermarket, France's answer to Sainsbury's. As I pushed my shopping trolley down the aisle to inspect the vast array of wonderful French cheeses, my cart accidentally came too close to a fat lady. Clad in a stained tank top and tight shorts with five inches of flab oozing over the top, she sported one of those amusing new haircuts, which consisted of half the head being shaved to the skull on the left side, and a hank of dyed black hair obscuring the other, including her right eye. She was yammering into her mobile, oblivious of anyone around. The creature's trolley was parked horizontally across the aisle and concealing a large part of the cheese counter, as she totally ignored everyone who tried to manoeuvre around her. When I attempted to peek over her vast shoulders for a glimpse of the Gruyère she hissed at me, 'Whaddaya want, bitch?' Quite taken aback, and wondering how she recognized my alter ego from the eponymous movie I had made, I stumbled back, stammering an apology. Why I should have said I'm sorry to a such sociopathic slag beats me but certainly the width and breadth of her enormity was rather intimidating, as was the gold tooth in the middle of her mouth, and the glowering hulk of a husband behind her.

Another time in a rather elegant boutique I picked out a shirt from the rack only to have it ripped from my hands by another woman. 'I saw it first!' she growled at me as I started to remonstrate. But then I smiled to myself, realizing that at 200lb she would never fit into a size 8!

Gone, gone, gone are the days when a gentleman lightly took your hand in his and brushed his lips across it, or tipped his hat to acknowledge you as he chivalrously stepped aside to let you pass. The very idea of opening a door for someone or standing up when a lady arrives at the table is completely unknown to most people today. Thanks to the liberation movement and the equality of the sexes we now have generations completely unaware of how to behave politely towards the fairer sex. Or even to one another!

I was lucky enough to grow up in a gentler era, when people queued politely and patiently in shops, at bus stops and theatres, when children had respect for their elders, particularly those authority figures like teachers or policemen, when no child would ever dream of addressing an adult by their Christian name unless they were asked to. Today, as young children seem unable to be controlled by their parents or teachers, not only has respect gone out with the parsley, as Michelle Pfeiffer observed in *The Fabulous Baker Boys*, but also good manners hardly seem to exist anywhere any more, except in the higher echelons of society or royalty, in our so-called civilized world.

It wasn't so long ago that Britain was a dangerous and terrifying place to live. Bandits and highwaymen roamed the country roads, and the city streets swarmed with pickpockets, thieves, con artists and brutal Bill-Sykes type villains. It was hazardous to walk through the crowded, stinking alleys and streets of London in the seventeenth, eighteenth and nineteenth centuries. Chamber pots were blithely emptied into the streets below, sometimes with a warning to 'watch the water' (hence the word 'loo', from the phrase *Gardez l'eau* and pronounced gardy-loo) but otherwise not – oblivious of the potentially unlucky target. Rabid dogs and cats roamed and scavenged, as did hundreds of thousands of rats, which infested the big of strangulated vowels and unable, due to what was expected of him socially, to show any kind of emotion. Overt displays of sentiment were frowned upon and the stiff upper lip of military legend became the normal way that the middle and upper classes behaved. But although perfectly well mannered in public, behind the respectable facades of the grand dwellings of the upper classes, all manner of bad behaviour was dished out to the disadvantaged who were mainly servants: practically the only jobs that the poor could aspire to. Servants in many grand houses lived in appalling conditions, were paid a paltry wage and were expected to be at their masters' and mistresses' bidding eighteen hours a day, six and a half days per week. They were severely punished for the slightest misdemeanour and the most distinguished of beautifully mannered noblemen would think nothing of dishing out the most horrendous punishments to any of their chattels, for that indeed is what they were considered to be. As were their wives. The servants were blamed for anything that went wrong, from fires that weren't burning brightly enough in every room, to the soup not being hot enough and even to their uniforms not being clean enough. (To add insult to injury, they had to pay for their uniforms out of their own wages.) The punishments would be anything from being chastised verbally, to being sent to bed without supper to, in extreme cases, violent corporal punishment. The masters controlled their servants totally, for the poor wretches knew if they were out on their ear there was nowhere for them to turn except the workhouse, if they were lucky, or to take to the streets if they were young and pretty.

There was no welfare state to cushion the conditions of the poor. Work in factories, mines or the dockyards was desperately hard and terribly ageing. A man of twenty could easily look forty. It behoved the workers to be extremely polite to their bosses who, although themselves polite and well mannered in equal company, usually treated the workers with callous indifference, tolerating nothing except submission. But to the outside world the bosses, merchants, upper classes, sires, lieges, chairmen – in other words, the ruling class – behaved in the most mannerly and courteous way to everyone in their circle.

But as the Industrial Revolution provided a better standard of living, and enlightened thinkers and writers created a more equal society, polite behaviour crossed class lines and became a unifying code for all strata of society. The period from around 1850 to the early 1960s was an *aspirational* time, where everyone strived towards the highest common denominator. However, in the last fifty years, the pendulum has swung so far the other way that now so many seem to be reaching for, or appealing to, the lowest common denominator. Sadly, this means we now appear to be going backwards and have more in common with our ancestors, the ravening hordes of Celts and blue-faced Britons that terrified the more enlightened Romans, rather than with the urbane and enlightened free thinkers who brought us out of that mire.

Speaking of ravening hordes, take for example the delightful habit of loutish young Brits flashing body parts at all and sundry when drunk during all seasons – holiday or not. The boys call it mooning and the girls 'flashing yer boobies'.

This now has caught on in the States, where in some places they are selling tapes online of mostly British youngsters on their Ibiza holidays, performing the degrading acts we've come to accept as commonplace. I was glad to hear that Nice has now passed a law forbidding anyone from going shirtless outdoors and that the police actually enforce it. The world might benefit from this example. My grandmother paid to take my mother to the *circus* to see the fat lady and the tattooed man but now you can see them for free whether you want to or not – they're all over the place.

I deplore the cult of yobbism. Why has the desire to eat, dress and talk properly become something to be scorned, a source of ridicule? You see vulgarity on the television, you see people sitting in restaurants, elbows on the table, boisterously drunk and talking loudly with open mouths full of food. Even the f-word, for example, now seems almost commonplace. My daughter Tara recently boarded a train at Paddington with her two young children. As the train left, about thirty boys and girls aged between fourteen and twenty-five climbed into Tara's first-class carriage and began berating her and her children using the foulest language. The children became terribly frightened as their assailants were all drunk and were angry and belligerent since their football team had lost. They couldn't care less that their f- and s- words were offensive and upsetting.

Eventually the conductor called the police who turfed them off at Reading but the unutterable rudeness and complete lack of consideration for all the people in the carriage was shocking. It has made Tara think twice about travelling by train again.

Aggressive behaviour is rife in the streets and on public transport, from people dressed in the sort of grungy clothes you wouldn't give to charity. Some American friends told me about a recent trip into London, where they were walking around in what they would regard as their normal clothes. They were set upon by a gang of youths who ridiculed them for being 'posh'. They were wearing well-cut expensive sportswear which they considered normal in LA. Why should wanting to look clean and nice and well-dressed trigger such hostility? The only explanation I can come up with unfortunately is envy.

I don't shout at somebody because they're dressed in dirty jeans and an old anorak. A new culture seems to have crept into our society, which applauds a lack of manners or politesse; which questions respect for the forces of law and order; which disregards the contribution that has been made by our senior citizens, those who fought the terrible threat of fascism and despotism – not because they were forced to and not because they weren't afraid and not because they didn't know any better – but because it was the *right thing to do for their country*.

Theirs was a generation which believed that if they didn't do the right thing, no matter how hard that may have been, they wouldn't have been able to face themselves in the morning. Now disparate swathes of our population, from benefit scroungers to respectable bankers, believe self-preservation is the only goal and must be achieved at the cost of the individuals who provide the means to achieve it. It's the 'me me me' generation.

Much of society in Britain in the nineties became so rude! We'd do well to stop and look back to learn some powerful lessons from the past before it's too late. I remember the fifties as being a wonderful decade. We'd come through a war. I was young and carefree. There was a great feeling of having beaten a terrible enemy and of a golden future lying ahead but that bright new future didn't unleash a wave of mindless selfishness, it became a spur to millions of ordinary people to make something of their lives after the privations they'd endured. Yet here we are over sixty years on, and where is the legacy of that hard-won freedom that our fathers and grandfathers fought for?

All too often today we read yet more sickening reports of defenceless old men or women having been beaten black and blue by some yob in search of a bit of cash. And when they record it on their mobile phones for mindless kicks it's even more horrible. Yobbism rules on too many sink estates and the weak judges and rules that empower the 'Oi've got me rights' types are ruining life for ordinary peace-loving people.

Why should anyone have to bring themselves down to the lowest common denominator merely to conform? The answer is one shouldn't, and I won't. But then I'm old enough now to be able to express my opinion without worrying about criticism, and to live the way I do and to know that the way I feel is the way many other people feel.

As a young girl, I could stroll around the streets of London, by night if I chose, and know that I'd be safe. That's no longer true. Today, my girls can't even walk down the street during the day without the possibility of something unpleasant happening. Catch someone's eye and you could be in trouble and if you are dressed elegantly and with some style you leave yourself open to being mocked, or worse still, mugged.

In spite of what many people might want to believe, the USA is still one of the most civilized places in the world. Generalizations are always tricky but I've found Americans for the most part charming, polite and extremely well mannered. The menacing yob culture we have in the UK seems not to have affected them in the same way, or even at all. One can go to a baseball, football or basketball game and enjoy it in relative peace without the horrible threat of a violent punch-up, fans screaming obscenities or the menacing presence of armed police and military supervision.

Luckily there are still small pockets of civilization left

in our great island. Attending the women's final at Wimbledon, it is a delight to watch tennis in adult and sophisticated surroundings – pray this never changes.

Yet even Americans have their faults. For example, I was just derided by a lady (I struggle to call her that) journalist in the *New York Post* for the way I said tomato, 'or "toe-mah-toh" as the British-born star pronounces it'. Can you imagine the Queen mocking someone's indigenous accent? She must meet thousands of different nationalities, some of whom must sound mighty strange attempting to emulate 'The Queen's English', but I am surprised by the number of Americans who make fun of even my slight accent. Of course, if I mocked a Texan or Hispanic or Brooklynite I'd probably be tarred and feathered and run out of town.

And the familiarity of so many people today! My blood runs cold when someone I've met maybe only once years ago sticks his or her face into mine and demands, 'Do you remember me?' This happens most often during the party season in Saint Tropez but can (and does) happen really anywhere in the world. Since I have a poor memory for faces (and some faces have been so plasticized that they're almost unrecognizable) I'm embarrassed when I forget the names of people I've met once or twice.

So now I have taken a leaf from Jack Nicholson's book, (certainly a face no one could forget). At parties he stretches out his hand and grins, 'Hi, I'm Jack,' which usually forces the other person to reveal their name. It also prevents that ghastly huggy, kissy performance which never fails to leave the female kisser's lipstick on either my cheek or jacket.

With the crush of the parties comes the crushing handshakes. Why do people – and I'm afraid it's usually men, although some women have also adopted this horrid habit – think that a bone crusher of a so-called civilized salute is requisite? Some theorize it's used to establish themselves as a 'solid citizen' whilst others argue it affirms their superiority over the crushee. I try not to shake hands at parties. Handbag in one, glass of wine in the other, I simply raise either in friendly salute and say 'hi'.

Sadly many dedicated hand-crunchers will refuse to accept this compromise and stand with their *manos* firmly extended. So I take a deep breath and extend a reluctant pinkie, resigned to being unable to wear my Theo Fennel ring for a week. I pity our dear Queen who has to cope with pulverizing handshakes constantly.

I do believe that some people receive a perverse pleasure from instead of shaking hands, squeezing your fingers so hard you are forced to let out a squawk of pain. I met a young lady from the Middle East recently who, when Percy extended his hand (he's a gentle hand-shaker, thanks to me) threw up her mitts in horror and squealed, 'My religion won't allow me to shake hands.' I'd like to try that one but I'd be hard-pressed to pass myself off as Muslim.

I was recently at an event in LA where a bunch of celebrities were being interviewed on a popular American TV programme. As I sat in the green room, Cindy

Crawford passed by with an entourage. She politely stopped to say hello and introduce her gaggle of PRs and make-up and hair people. One of the ladies extended a hand and when I put mine out likewise she closed it over my knuckles in a vice-like grip reminiscent of the handshake I'd received from Arnold Schwarzenegger. My yelp of pain reverberated across the concourse and there was a pause in the milling crowd as they turned their heads to find out where the wail was coming from. 'Sorry,' I said in embarrassment at their stupefied faces, 'but that hurt!' She gave me a pitying look but, hey, I'm a lady – I have no desire to compete in an arm-wrestling match to determine my strength.

At Selfridges 100th anniversary a girl dashed forward to greet me in hug'n'kiss mode, arms akimbo. Lips pursed, I took a step back and said, 'Sorry, I don't kiss people I don't know.' The paparazzi loved it because the girl in question was one Lily Allen, whom I had never met. Later that night she went on Twitter to report that I had blanked her! By next morning friends in America were emailing me about this (to me) non-event. It used to be the power of the press. Now it's the power of Twitter or Facebook, which leads me to that other realm of bad manners – the Internet and technology, yet another element eroding the last bastion of politesse.

I used to think that tweeting was just for the birds but now there seems to be an epidemic of people peck, peck, pecking away at their iPhones, BlackBerries, Strawberries or whatevers. Whilst I myself also tweet and I do consider that in the right time and place it can be an invaluable form of communication (e.g. revolutions, strikes, the Royal Wedding etc.), it can be especially irritating when, at a dinner party or restaurant, someone has their hands under the table trying to hide the fact their thumbs are hard at work. Many tweeters seem to care not for the people they're supposed to be socializing with as they punch in those 140 characters informing whoever cares that they are 'On the train now', or 'Having a bit of a lie down', or 'reading Joan's new book'.

At an Oscar party last year, I turned to my right to start a conversation, only to find my dinner partner tap, tap, tapping away, and, as I looked across the table at Percy, found he was equally surrounded by tweeters. I then turned to my left, only to find my other dinner companion also entranced by his keypad. Defeated, I ordered another martini, and sat back to watch the ceremony on the dozens of TV screens set up around us – I was surrounded by technology and with no visible means of escape!

I am stumped that so many people are addicted to technology, even though I confess that I do enjoy it. But when you're seated near Kirk Douglas, Jay Leno, Jane Fonda, Jackie Collins and you prefer to hunch over your tiny screen, sharing your thoughts with other people, go figure.

I do lay the blame for much of our failing values squarely at the door of so-called progress. I learned to read before I was five and I then used that ability to devour as many books as I could lay my hands on. How different it might have been for me as a child if I had had an endless diet of videos on which to gorge, or any number of different TV channels to surf without even having to move from my chair.

When I was a child, going to the cinema, the theatre or a concert was an exciting event precisely because it was a rarity, a treat. Now, with so much entertainment available at the flick of a switch, kids have become jaded and easily bored. Look at any young person in a family restaurant. From the age of four and up they are glued to a mobile or a video game.

This constant fixation with being glued to screens is downright rude, not to mention unhealthy. So many of us now spend too many hours in front of computers and TV screens or on mobile phones and as a result have become completely numb to what is going on in the real world. When I was performing in the panto *Dick Whittington* recently, I was told it was necessary now for all performers to wear microphones so we could be heard above the din of the deafening music and special effects that constituted our background, simply because the audiences at home, accustomed to their over-amplified home theatre systems, demand it.

'But I can project enough,' I complained. I hate body microphones. You're trussed up like a hog off to market. Big wires are stuck on your cheek, then wound around your ears and hang out the back of your clothes attached to a heavy mic pack bigger than a cigarette pack. This in turn has to be attached around your waist with a thick belt under your outfit. It's torturous.

When I was performing in *Private Lives* in New York with Simon Jones, my co-star had his microphone under his toupee on his forehead because the system kept shorting out and sometimes you would hear a police announcement: 'Forced entry at 46th St and Lexington – car 32 to report immediately.' It was hard not to laugh. Mae West wore an earpiece in *Myra Breckinridge* through which someone would say her lines to her, which she would then repeat. When she spouted out 'runaway car on the freeway; all personnel to follow', the whole crew collapsed in laughter. Sadly Mae didn't see the funny side.

Along with the loss of etiquette comes the loss of interesting, witty conversation that is not laced with a stream of epithets that would make sailors blanch. When the controversial Kenneth Tynan uttered the f-word for the first time ever on TV in 1965 all hell broke loose. It was as shocking to hear this word said out loud as it would have been, in olden days, to reveal a glimpse of stocking, as Cole Porter wrote. Now, even actresses receiving Oscars say it and even if the television bleeps it out they seem to feel little embarrassment.

As a child I had never even heard the f-word, so it was only when I saw it written on the wall of a railway carriage that I enquired, 'Mummy, what does f*** mean?' The poor darling went ballistic, hissing, 'That is the most terrible word in the English language and if your father ever used it I would divorce him!' A touch of overkill I suspect but since my grandmother was of course a Victorian, my mother was brought up with those strict moral values.

These must have trickled down in some way to me too, because I must admit that I'm often appalled at the offensiveness and coarseness that passes for dialogue in the last decade on many of our TV programmes. It seems to have trickled down in real life too. Should anyone dare complain, 'freedom of speech' is paraded out and the person guilty of finding gratuitous foul language and actions offensive, or refusing to speak about their sex lives or bathroom habits is branded either an old fogey, a prude or hopelessly old fashioned. The c-word was considered *verboten* for years and I still consider it a nasty epithet and demeaning to women, but Gwyneth Paltrow said it several times on TV recently, referring to her grandmother. It seems it's more acceptable now to use that word than to call somebody fat.

I was glad that the BBC censured the obscene and degrading actions of Russell Brand and Jonathan Ross against Andrew Sachs. Suspending Ross and forcing foul-mouthed Brand to resign was a brave move on the part of the Beeb, which too often contributes to, rather than opposes, the decline of standards in television programming. However, they acted only *after* receiving thousands of complaints and having Parliament on their backs.

I have stopped watching many TV shows because the

unfunny, crude, rude and lavatorial humour leaves me cold. Many British entertainers used to be known for their sophisticated, sly wit and their stylish or ironic *bon mots*. It is sadly no longer true. How horrible was a Comedy Roast on Channel 4 for dear Bruce Forsyth, when a bunch of no-name, so-called comics made fun of our national treasure while spewing out insults, obscenity and filth?

It seems that the more profanity a comedian can spit out in one sentence, the more people laugh for some idiotic reason. Wit and true humour are only to be found on the American nightly talk shows of Jay Leno, David Letterman and Jon Stewart. All of them are exceedingly amusing and rarely, if ever, resort to four-letter words and filthy innuendo. Of course the US networks have a very strict code on swearing and lavatorial humour is frowned upon. Yet they manage to achieve consistent comedy night after night, year after year. Could Ross and Brand do the same?

Like most people, what really makes me laugh is that increasingly scarce commodity, true wit. By that I don't mean the 'hilarious anecdote', constantly repeated which has been honed and polished to perfection from years of repetition. I mean real wit, which hits the mark with such speed that it renders those who hear it dumbstruck for a couple of seconds. I was at a dinner with Adrian Gill, who was regaling our guests with his experiences in America, writing and directing a porno movie. He was explaining that two versions of the same film are shot at almost the same time – one 'soft', the other 'hard'. Apparently, while they were shooting the soft version, the commonly heard complaint from an assistant crouched over a monitor was 'Hey, move the camera down, I'm getting ball-sack.'

'What's that?' I asked naively.

Without missing a beat, one of our friends replied, 'A French writer.'

So who can blame today's youth for not having good manners if one looks at the fare provided by television, movies and the Internet? If programming is a reflection of our society and in turn informs and educates people as to how to behave, then the future is hopeless. Surfing the morning chat shows, I'm horribly fascinated by the dysfunctional weirdoes dominating both American and British airwaves. On Jeremy Kyle's squawk show, few of his guests are not circumferentially, or indeed mentally challenged. In their clownish costumes of tight leggings, baggy T-shirts and enormous trainers they are real-life Dumbos. Nothing seems too gross to shock any more. 'My pimp runs my family', 'I made love to my mother's boy-friend while she watched' and 'I'm twelve and have unprotected sex' are just some of the salacious subjects that help to sell their programmes. On Mr Kyle's show nothing is left to the imagination. As these grotesques air their dirty linen I quickly change channels. They seem to let it all hang out, but at odds with this is the unwritten law of political correctness, which still reigns supreme. Although dozens of subjects are considered politically incorrect, it seems that bad language and discussion of bodily functions are not. Unfortunately, this is spreading beyond the realm of Jeremy Kyle – at a BAFTA awards I attended a so-called comedian informed those of us in the audience, 'I'm so nervous, my pants are full.' What a charming visual image.

Does anyone really care about the half-baked celebrities and wannabes on *Big Brother* who whip off their clothes at the drop of a hat and indulge in wretched 'hide and seek' sex under duvets while pretending not to be aware of the camera? This genre has spawned masses of similar programmes, which follow the daily lives of various D-list celebs and are nauseating in their detail yet are simultaneously unbelievably boring. It amuses me to see the efforts of the producers, who even hire fake paparazzi to make these simpletons look far more important than they are. There are far too many of these so-called reality shows on the air: celebrity chefs galore effing and blinding across kitchens nationwide, husbands and wives swapping partners with each other, parents in despair handing over unruly, spoiled children to a 'super nanny', and everyone pushing the boundaries to get to the lowest common denominator of bad taste.

I am quite impressed when some young person displays a degree of polish simply because it is so rare nowadays. Strangely, too, I find that the older some people become, the more amnesic they are with manners. Often the worst offenders are men over fifty, who barge past you in the queue, grab your seat on public transport, refusing to budge, arms akimbo, as you try to pass them on the pavement. Meeting my husband at a café in Saint Tropez recently after shopping I found that the seat he'd been holding for me had been taken. When Percy politely asked the man who had borrowed my seat to return it, the old codger simply turned his back and ignored us, leaving me standing with six heavy shopping bags. Percy immediately stood to offer me his seat and fortunately a well-mannered waiter noticed our plight and hurried to bring me a chair, hauling it over the head of the man who continued to pretend not to notice me.

The perfect spot for seeing the complete and utter destruction of manners is at the airport. Everyone is so completely dehumanized by the experience of being rushed and prodded past security lines, check-in lines and generally treated like cattle going to the abattoir that the descent to numbness can be forgiven. Everyone is in a mindless hurry and seems to have blinkers on so that they aren't aware of anyone else. At Gatwick one needs earplugs too, such is the cacophony of squealing kids, screaming jets, garbled loudspeaker announcements and piped pop music.

Passengers rush about in a daze bumping into each other like pin-balls with their pesky little wheelies, which become lethal weapons. At JFK a few years ago, whilst Percy was getting our bags, I was attempting to save my two-year-old toddler granddaughter Ava from being run over by a luggage trolley. As I bent over to grab her, a tourist from Hong Kong slammed her ton-sized wheeled suitcase right into the back of my ankles. I fell to the ground, hitting my knees hard on the floor and as I cried in pain she yelled, 'You should get out of my way.' With no regard for my wellbeing, she rushed off leaving me doubled up on the floor clutching a wailing infant. Not one person came near me to enquire if I was OK, and the severe pain in my Achilles heel lasted for eighteen months! Is the moral of this story then that everyone should fend for themselves, or should people try not to be so damned self-involved?

First there was road rage, then air rage, and now I've witnessed a new phenomenon close-up: shopping rage. My friend Jack Rich, who like me majored *summa cum laude* in shopping, accompanied me for a day of boutique browsing, which we liken to fun fishing trips. We spent twenty minutes with a salesperson in a Fifth Avenue store, carefully selecting various items, then followed him to an empty till where he began totting up our catch. 'Hey, man, what the hell are y'doing?' yelled an angry voice from the back of the queue behind the other till. The salesman muttered that he'd been helping us, and started to ring up my purchases. 'Hey, hey, hey, you must be star-struck, man. We was here first. Let her get in line behind us.' I turned to see a very big, very angry young man with a chip on his shoulder the size of Texas. My glance seemed to enrage him even more as, oozing fury, he continued to berate the hapless clerk: 'Get me the manager. You ring that store manager right now, d'you hear?' The five poor wretches in front of him hung their heads in embarrassment, trying to pretend that they weren't there, while the clerk continued totting. 'You're a star-f—er, that's what you are, a f—ing star-f—er!' The man was rabid by now. If he'd been a dog, he'd have been foaming at the mouth. I didn't need to hear any more venom. Any second I expected a .45 to be pulled, and I could see the headlines: 'Actress Dies in Shopping Shoot-out'. I grabbed Jack's arm, my plastic from the clerk, and we hastily left the building. Not out of cowardice, but I simply wouldn't be caught dead in Gap!

I think it is a tremendous tragedy that we have sunk so low in such a relatively short space of time. But then I actually read an article in a left-wing paper the other day that said it was wrong to give Winston Churchill so much credit for helping us win the war. Dear God. When I was a schoolgirl, Winston Churchill was the greatest hero this country had ever produced. And President Obama's decision to remove the Winston Churchill bust from the White House as penance for the persecution of his great-grandfather (never mind that we had abolished slavery and fiercely policed the waves of Britannia in search of *American* slave traders long before their Civil War) was a churlish act. The bust is now in the British Ambassador's residence.

I'm totally on the side of family life. I was lucky enough to grow up in a loving household and, although I have been divorced, it never would have occurred to me to have any of my three children out of wedlock. I'm becoming more and more convinced that the disintegration of the nuclear family mirrors the disintegration of our society.

Having a child is the greatest responsibility anyone can take on. It has always struck me as odd that, whereas you used to need a licence to have a dog, the same was not true of having a child. I thought very, very hard indeed before I had my first child. Indeed, I had an abortion in my twenties because, after much soul-searching, I wasn't convinced that my relationship with the father would endure – and I believed that was an unsound basis for bringing a child into the world.

I'm sure I shall be criticized for expressing my views. But I'm sure, too, that I express many of the views of a silent majority in Britain today. My heart goes out to all the ordinary, decent people who work hard to make something of their lives for themselves and their children and who pay their taxes uncomplainingly. They're the ones – as Marilyn Monroe once said – who are getting the fuzzy end of the lollipop. All of which probably makes me sound reactionary, conservative and rather old-fashioned. But do you know something? I couldn't care less. To quote the gifted American historian and philosopher, Will Durant, 'A great civilization is not conquered from without until it has destroyed itself from within.' But I really hope that this is not happening to our great country.

On Ageing:
It's Better than the Alternative

If we're lucky enough to enjoy longer life expectancies, most people can expect to be middle-aged and older for the majority of their lives. So why does society insist that the old are useless?

In the plot of a movie called *Logan's Run*, everyone was 'terminated' after the age of thirty in a bizarre ritual. Judging from the perspective of the media and society in general, maybe we're not far off that: 'Live fast, die young, leave a good-looking corpse,' says John Derek in the 1949 film, *Knock on Any Door*. Well, I don't want to live fast but I don't want to die young either because there is still a lot I want to enjoy in life. I use the word 'older' because I believe that while we may become older, we do not have to *become* old.

Women finally became emancipated more than ninety years ago when we won the right to vote. We were on the road to equality and we obtained respect, certainly in the Western world. But in spite of that, for several decades women have had to endure a more insidious form of discrimination – that of ageism.

Men now on average can expect to reach the age of seventy-seven and women eighty-one, which is amazing when you consider that in Victorian Britain the average life expectancy was forty-eight, and fifty-four for women, who by forty would have been considered worn-out old crones. Only the very rich managed to survive into middle age. Then by 1946 practically everyone could expect to hit the golden age of sixty-seven. In a century and a half from the Victorian era, life expectancy has increased by over fifty years – imagine what it could rise to in another fifty?

So why are men and many women in their forties and fifties, who now may have another forty or more years of living ahead of them, considered 'past it'?

The population of the world is changing. In the UK, in the period spanning twenty-five years from 1984 to 2009, the percentage of the population aged sixty-five or over increased from 15 to 16 per cent. Over the same period, the percentage of the population aged under sixteen decreased from 21 to 19 per cent. This trend is projected to continue. By 2034, 23 per cent of the population is expected to be aged sixty-five and over compared to 18 per cent under age sixteen. So why is it that as birth rates fall the greater portion of people who are now over sixty do not have a proper place in society and are often considered worthless, our potential contributions deemed inconsequential?

Yet manufacturers and advertisers cling to that '18-39' demographic as if it were the oracle that will guarantee a rosy future.

'Ageing' is a horrible word often used by the media in the most derogatory way: 'ageing rock star'; 'ageing actress'. It's almost as if the word is used to denote uselessness.

Face it, folks, ageing begins at the moment of birth and ends when life ends and we must make the most of every minute. People always searched for the fountain of youth, which has often represented immortality, yet now it literally means youth. You are judged no longer by how young you *look* and act but by how old you actually *are*.

At the age of twenty I was contracted to 20th Century Fox in Hollywood and the PR man, whilst writing my bio, asked, 'Wouldn't you rather say you're eighteen?'

'That's ridiculous,' I said. 'Everyone I went to school with will know I am lying.'

'It's surprising how many actresses will snip a few years off,' he laughed. 'You're the exception to the rule.'

When I was thirty-nine I played a glamorous courtesan in a TV mini-series; however, my agent had told the producers I was thirty-two. When the producer discovered how old I really was he told me point blank, 'I'd never have hired you if I'd known.'

'But why?' I asked. 'I was still being asked for ID until a couple of years ago.'

'Because,' he said, 'the public wants to see only *young* people in sexy, glamorous roles.'

I mentioned an actor who was never short of work at the time, but who looked much older than he actually was. The producer said, 'It doesn't matter because he's a man.'

'Oh wow – ageism is alive and well, and living in Hollywood,' I laughed. I'm glad I shaved off a few years.

Whilst sitting with Sir John Gielgud at a press junket for a TV show called *Neck*, a reporter popped the overused question, 'How old are you, Joan?'

Gielgud looked up from *The Times* crossword angrily. 'Young man, *never* ask an actress her age. Actors are victims of our physicality – do you think Dame Edith Evans would have been able to play a fourteen-year-old Juliet if everyone knew she was thirty-two? We are an illusion! Let's try and leave it that way.'

'Thanks, darling,' I said. 'Does that mean you couldn't play the gardener in that script I sent you?'

'My dear, I could *never* play a gardener – look at these hands,' he held out smooth manicured hands. 'Are these the hands of a gardener?'

'You could wear gloves,' I ventured.

'Gloves!! A gardener! No my dear, we actors must realize our limitations in terms of our physical looks –

that is why you, my dear, could never play an ugly or plain woman.'

'I could try – with make up and prosthetics,' I said.

Sir John laughed. 'You won't be believable.'

As it turned out he was completely correct because although I did play several unglamorous roles on television, Alexis put the kibosh on me going grungy and most directors and casting people don't see me in that light.

I did try to take a few years off my age during the filming of *The Stud*, when I told the publicity people that I was three years younger than I was. The *News of the World* went to Somerset House and dug up my birth certificate, which they printed on the front page with a booming headline – JOAN LIES ABOUT HER AGE! You would think I had murdered a family of four. Despite being one of the few actresses who has been 'outed' in such a public and shameful way, there are still people who believe I'm lying about my age. I can't think of anyone else who has been so deeply and thoroughly probed on this issue than me.

However much actresses Botox and plasticize themselves, however young they look, it's still their *age* that matters to the moguls in LALA land. Because no one sees beyond the number, this attitude permeates everywhere, from the factory to the office, the boardroom to fashion.

Fashion and celebrity magazines are the greatest perpetrators of the 'youth is the only thing that matters' phenomenon. One of America's most famous and revered designers announced recently, 'I am *only* interested in dressing women under age forty who are at least five feet eight inches tall, weigh no more than 120 pounds and have a thirty-two-inch bust.'

But how many women can aspire to *that*?

It distresses me to see so many ghastly Botoxed and 'filled' faces on women today. Many women, quite a few of them actresses, look really strange with their 'pillow' lips, puffed-up cheeks and fake cheekbones, which makes their eyes look like tiny pits in a marshmallow cloud.

I cannot understand why women want to fill their faces with a toxin that paralyses muscles and with fillers that have not been properly tested because there are still no absolute guarantees that these procedures are not harmful.

What these products claim they *can* do compared to the list of what can go wrong is alarming: allergic reactions; persistent swelling and inflammation; weird lumps that appear around the face and sometimes excruciating migraines. I just don't think it's worth it.

When articles are written about me or any of my contemporaries who have had the good fortune and discipline to look good at *un age certain*, I am struck by the tone of astonishment and the certainty that *something* is being done, or has been done, *secretly* to beat the clock.

People (particularly press people) often comment on the fact that I always wear make-up and that's why I don't have many wrinkles. Well, the fact is that make-up only *exacerbates* wrinkles; it certainly doesn't hide them. The reason that people think I wear a lot of make-up is that I have good skin. And why is this? Because I've *always* protected my face from the elements with foundation, moisturizer and a hat to keep the sun off my visage. Some women don't realize that the sun's rays can get through even the gloomiest day, which is why I always wear a protective base – and SPF.

But why *should* the media be surprised that women of any age can still be good-looking and sexy? Unfortunately, with the media's excessive emphasis on youth, youth, youth, many women over forty begin to feel unsexy and insecure. With recent news that women over forty-six become 'invisible' to men, it isn't really surprising that some women will go to any length to stop the clock. Today there are thousands women looking stunning and far younger than their biological age and there are dozens of actresses over a certain age who look great and are an inspiration: Sophia Loren, Helen Mirren, Joanna Lumley, Stephanie Powers, Linda Grey. . . . These are just a few names from an endless list – and these are just the actresses! What about the scores of elegant models including Inès de La Fressange, Linda Evangelista, Claudia Schiffer, Elle Macpherson, Iman, Christie Brinkley and many more; all gorgeous and youthfully vibrant.

This idea that older women should not or cannot be sexy is absurd. This obsession with youth is actually an Anglo thing. In France they revere and respect older women, as they do in most Latin countries, where they appreciate the delightful allure of confident older women.

But let's not forget the importance of sex. Many of the most famous women were sexually active well into middle age and beyond. The great French actress Sarah Bernhardt and the legendary Coco Chanel both had lovers well into their later lives. Catherine the Great was reputed to have taken younger lovers (and the odd horse) to bed. Mae West, who lived to ninety, had a live-in lover forty-five years younger than she was, and she coined the classic phrase: 'It's not the men in my life, but the life in my men'. When asked how she kept herself looking so young, she replied: 'I go to bed early, I meditate, I eat all the right foods, I don't smoke or drink alcohol and I believe in myself with a passion. You can only beat nature when you show the bitch who's boss!'

There's another challenge women of today face – it's called 'computerface' and it's becoming more and more prevalent as women spend endless hours hunched over computers. Beauticians say they are seeing far too much of this. Working long hours in front of a computer screen can give women (and men – maybe even kids) 'turkey neck', saggy jowls and deep wrinkles on their foreheads and their eyes. Many doctors report that sitting down for long periods of time, staring at a screen, makes the neck muscles stronger and they will eventually start to sag. When women are stressed or concentrating they tend to frown and screw up their face. Try placing a mirror next to your computer and you'll see all the different expressions you make. It's scary!

Many young people think that sex is their own prerogative and are appalled by the idea of the over-forties, or even their parents, being or looking sexy or even, God forbid, having sex. This is almost a throwback to days of puritanical religious intolerance, when sex was only meant for reproduction. I believe we have come far beyond those beliefs in our new secular age, and even in some parts of the religious one as well. Now that sex is used to sell everything from vacuum cleaners (painful but true) to plane tickets it should be accepted that it is every adult's prerogative to enjoy it and have it. It delights me to read about a couple marrying in their eighties, or redis-covering their lost love from fifty years ago. Romance never dies if you believe in it.

I have friends in their sixties, seventies and even eighties not in the limelight who all look absolutely stunning. They all have one thing in common: they have taken care of themselves all their lives by eating a reason-ably healthy diet, exercising moderately and not allowing themselves to become overweight. Excess weight is one of the most ageing and unhealthy things that can happen to anyone (discussed in my chapter on food). The current life expectancy of eighty-five years for women actually translates to many more years if she continues basic maintenance and, of course, doesn't become ill. Sadly, many of today's illnesses stem from being overweight and the body having to lug around too much extra *avoirdupois*.

Boring as it is, I exercise at least three times a week. I call my trainer Tonya 'the Tiny Torturer', and nag her relentlessly as she forces me to do those extra fifty crunches or yet another brisk walk. But I see some women around my age who are completely bedridden or wheelchair-bound and I *know* that if only they had taken just a little bit better care of themselves they could be so much fitter and more active.

I feel little different now from when I was in my forties and I put most of that down to discipline, without being fanatical in terms of exercise and food consumption. And of course my happy gene, which frankly I put down to the luck of the draw.

You are only truly 'young' for less than one third of your life, which means that for a good portion of our lifespan we women are classified by that horrid epithet: 'older woman'. But I agree with that great philosopher Bernard Baruch who said, 'Old age is always fifteen years older than I am'; or with Groucho Marx, who said, 'Growing old is something you do if you're lucky'. And then there was the director Billy Wilder – when he was ninety, someone asked him, 'Who the hell wants to be ninety-five?' 'Someone who's ninety-four!' he quipped.

The late Queen Mother was a fabulous example of living life to the fullest until well over a hundred, and having plenty of admirers, too. I met the Queen Mother several times, and she was a great *Dynasty* fan as she told me when I was presented to her at a London premiere.

'Oh dear, don't you hate me?' I asked.

'Oh no, my dear, we love you,' she said, smiling.

'You will never be as young or as good-looking as you are today'. Anyone who worries about getting older should adopt this mantra, along with 'I may not like getting older, but it's better than the alternative', or 'So what if I'm getting older, many are denied the privilege'. Mantras are useful to keep sight of what is important, mainly that 'life is a banquet, and most poor suckers are starving to death'. Jokes, too, keep things in perspective: 'You're so old you think a BlackBerry is a fruit.'

Since 'fifty is now the new thirty' then seventy should now be considered the new fifty and therefore, sponsors and advertisers need to court the fifty-plus market, because this group are not averse to doing everything younger people do, such as enjoying sex, looking good, having fun, decorating their homes, going on lavish holidays – the list is endless and they have the disposable income with which to do it.

And the argument that older people don't change brands or go for innovative products is absolute balder-dash when you consider that the iPad is the single most popular mobile device in the world right now and that the *largest demographic of iPad users are in the 35–60+ age group*. I love mine, and although I never learned to type, I'm a dab hand with one finger.

I have been aware since my twenties that youth is one of the most prized commodities, particularly for women.

On Ageing

I was told categorically by a producer at the age of seventeen, when I started in films, that 'You'd better make all the money you can because by the time you're twenty-five you'll be washed up'. At twenty-six or twenty-seven, most actresses were considered past their prime, and the search constantly revolved around finding the next nubile starlet to fill the shoes of the poor old faded ones pushing thirty. If you don't believe me, just ask yourself whatever happened to Geena Davis, Debra Winger or Kim Basinger. Even talented and sexy actresses like Demi Moore and Sharon Stone don't get leading roles any more.

When you consider that in an average film or TV drama at least 75 per cent of the roles are for men, it's understandable that there are so few roles for women today. Since so much entertainment is geared towards an audience of males between the ages of fourteen to twenty-eight, it's also understandable that they only want to see cute, skinny girls on the screen and so that is what the bosses at the networks and the studios aim for. With the exception of Meryl Streep and Judy Dench, and in France, Catherine Deneuve, there are sadly few actresses over fifty consistently working today.

I kept wondering why this was, when I became a groundbreaker on *Dynasty* and then posed tastefully nude for *Playboy* magazine at the age of forty-nine. Then I realized that to attain stardom and sexual allure after the age of thirty-five had simply not been done before on such a global scale. I am now extremely proud of my

171

accomplishments and am happy when asked to sign the now collectors' item the *Playboy* issue has become!

My parents and their contemporaries often referred to any unmarried woman over thirty-five as a 'dried-up old spinster'. I determined this wasn't going to happen to little ol' me. I was lucky enough to have been dealt a good hand from the genetic pool: apart from my mother, who tragically died of breast cancer in her mid-fifties, I knew that most of my female relatives lived well into their comparatively healthy eighties, as did my father.

I realized, however, that there was no point in living to a ripe old age if I wasn't in tip-top health, mentally and physically, so I started to address that issue by having regular physical check ups, particularly mammograms and following some other useful mantras:

You are what you eat
My mother had always stressed the importance of a nutritious diet, so I was lucky enough not to be fed junk food, which practically didn't exist when I was a child. Instead, I was made to consume goodly portions of fresh greens, milk, eggs, liver (yes!), fish and fruit. My parents rightfully believed that too much sugar was bad for you and ruined one's appetite. As a result, chocolates and sweets were rare and very special treats. How is it that they knew all these things before the modern proliferation of healthy-living articles and books? I guess it was just good old-fashioned common sense.

When I was pregnant in the mid-sixties and then in

the seventies, I told my obstetricians that I was going to give my babies the best start in life because I was taking vitamin supplements. I had read Victor Lindlahr's book *You Are What You Eat*, which was first published in 1940 and focused on the right foods and the power of supplements, which I began to take religiously. To my extreme dismay, the doctor pooh-poohed this idea, telling me that my babies would receive all the necessary nutrients if I followed 'a balanced diet'. He gave me a chart, which basically gave me carte blanche to eat anything I wanted, which I *knew* was wrong – for me and for my baby. If I'd consumed six slices of wholemeal bread and four glasses of milk a day plus endless portions of fruit, vegetables and meat, I would have turned into a barrage balloon and still not had all the vitamins my baby needed to grow strong and healthy.

I truly believe that vitamin supplements are essential, particularly as you get older, and I know they can prevent many different kinds of illnesses. From the age of forty my father suffered from dreadfully debilitating arthritis in his fingers and hands so I take several vitamin supplements to prevent it. MSM is brilliant for keeping joints supple, as is Vitamin E and Maxepa, an Omega-3 capsule I can't live without. So far I've been able to keep my father's ghost at bay. Calcium supplements are also essential, so I chew these tablets several times a day, as I dread the thought of osteoporosis. Thankfully, I have very strong bones (possibly in part due to taking the tablets), as I've had several falls onstage in the past couple of years and sustained nothing more than bruising. I'm certain that good health is not only due to genetics, but also to the supplements I take, and the foods I eat or don't eat.

Use it or lose it
Of course, exercise is crucial to healthy living. Although I'm not a fan of heavy exercise and aerobics, as I believe that after a certain age it weakens the body, I do work-out several times a week, and do Pilates and swimming when possible, not simply for the cosmetic benefits but because I want to be able to do whatever I could do twenty, thirty or even forty years ago. The fast food, binge-boozing, drug-taking and promiscuous sexual attitude that so many fifteen- to twenty-five-year-olds indulge in is going to make them prematurely aged and suffer serious health ailments in later life.

I recently spent the weekend at a health farm and underwent rigorous physical testing to determine my physiological age. It involved measuring flexibility, lung capacity, heart rate, strength, et cetera. I was thrilled when the instructor handed me the results, which revealed that my physiological age was forty-three!

'Wow, Percy, I'm younger than you!' I gloated to my forty-five-year-old husband, who groaned and said, 'Yes, I know. It's hard for me to keep up with you.'

You get the body and the face you deserve
Time and again I see women over forty who have taken care of themselves and look fabulous and in contrast girls

in their twenties and thirties who look, to be kind, rather rough. Maintenance needn't be time-consuming. Protecting one's skin with sunscreen and foundation takes as long as cleaning your teeth thoroughly. Doing twenty minutes of stretching, light weights and floor exercises three times a week takes the same amount of time as a long coffee break and eating a freshly made tuna-fish salad, sardines on toast or scrambled eggs is surely preferable to a Big Mac or KFC. It's not a question of being obsessive to look and feel good – I'm not – it's about doing it so regularly that it becomes almost second nature, like brushing one's teeth. I don't deprive myself –I eat chocolates, cookies and nuts; I drink wine and the occasional vodka tonic; but I quit smoking. It's simply about being sensible and not overindulging. I have treated my body as I would my car. Only the best petrol, care and maintenance for my vintage Rolls – same for me!

The world today is now filled with possibilities our parents couldn't have dreamed of. The over-fifties have begun to care less about our age and more about the type of person we are – and let our energy, ideas and lifestyle define who and what we are. For various reasons, we are much more curious and youthful in our outlook. Thus a person in their seventies and someone in their forties are more readily able to bond and share similar outlooks and values. I'm glad to see that many so-called ageing men and women are better dressed and groomed and more amusing and at ease with themselves than those who are decades younger. I just wish that advertisers and the media would come to realize this, also.

Some tips on looking after your body

As we become older, every part of our body needs more attention, particularly our bones, which become more brittle with age.

Remember, we all fall down the minute we start to walk. As I watched my children as toddlers take their first steps, it seemed that they fell down at least a dozen times a day, yet never seemed to get bruised. As a young mother my heart was in my mouth several times a week as little Tara tumbled out of her high chair, or Sacha climbed a tree in the garden and fell on to his head. On one particular occasion, his three-second silence before he started yelling was one of the most chilling experiences of my life. With extreme youth, bouncing back from falls is easy, but as the decades roll on it can be decidedly dangerous. There is *nothing* more ageing than having to walk with a stick, being in a wheelchair, or pushing a walker or Zimmer frame. While a cast covered in graffiti can look cute on a ten-year-old, on an adult it just looks sad.

The most prevalent causes of accident and death in the over sixty-fives is linked to falls. Whereas a broken arm in a twelve-year-old will mend in weeks, the arm of a seventy-year-old can take much, much longer to heal, be far more painful and lead to muscular atrophy and the acceleration of overall mental and physical deterioration.

Therefore, if you want to continue to look and feel young as you age, it is imperative to protect yourself from falls and accidents, and protect those bones.

I once had a ridiculous injury to my toe in a hotel. I broke it by gently bumping my unshod foot against a metal table leg. It was painful and infuriating, as broken toes cannot be set, and I was forced to endure months of fitting my foot into bigger-size shoes and hobbling around as best I could. It was odd that such a tiny bump caused this break because a few years later I performed in a panto, which involved a great deal of running about on stage, dancing, being lifted by five boys and walking up and down steep steps. I felt great, had no aches or pains, and was full of energy.

In Britain there are more than 35,000 serious injuries caused by falls each year. Women over sixty-five account for around 30 per cent of those injured and for men over sixty-five the figure is closer to 20 per cent. Three-quarters of them become seriously hurt. As we age, vision, balance, reflexes and hearing are not as spot-on as they were, and this leads to a heightened possibility of a fall. My late friend Eva Gabor broke her hip in Mexico, contracted pneumonia due to her weakened condition and died shortly afterwards, and this was a terrifically vibrant woman who had the best care.

Osteoporosis afflicts nearly 20 per cent of people over sixty. Many doctors advise a bone-density scan after the age of fifty to check if osteoporosis is developing. If so, there are calcium treatments and pills that can keep it in check and you should also talk to your doctor as to whether an anti-pneumonia inoculation would be advisable.

To continue feeling youthful, physical activity of any kind is absolutely essential. Walking, going to the gym, swimming and using free weights, which build muscle strength, are a must. I have a couple of friends who have virtually taken to their beds from the age of sixty and with each passing year they are more frail and feeble, and even though they are overweight, the rolls of fat won't protect them from breaking something when they fall, which they do regularly. They were both beautiful women, but sadly they are no longer.

One of the other reasons for falls amongst the older generation is that many are required to take a variety of pills for a variety of ailments, and these have side-effects including dizziness, forgetfulness and sleeplessness, which all contribute to a lack of balance.

However, if you're on medication and can't do as much exercise as you'd like, and if your doctor OKs it, or during those times when you know you are operating well, you can still aim to keep your body tuned up. Walk faster if you can and always take the stairs rather than the lift whenever possible, even if it's only for a few flights. And stretch for at least five minutes when you wake up in the mornings to stimulate your body, which will help keep it trim and supple. Animals do it when they wake up – look at a cat!

Have you noticed how lethargic your body feels after a few days in bed with a cold or flu? Your legs seem to have lost their power, you feel weak and frail and your lungs can't cope with walking, let alone running or swimming. This is a very minor state of atrophy, but if you can imagine months or years of not using your body you can visualize how weak and enfeebled you will become. Prevention is preferable to a cure. So stay on your feet and do what you can to prevent becoming another Humpty-Dumpty! Creaky bones, difficulty in moving and slow, ponderous steps are terribly ageing.

The more you exercise, the better your body will become. But you can't overdo it. Unless you have been used to exerting yourself with a physical regime for years, from middle-age or even earlier, you *cannot* start running ten miles a day or begin lifting 200lb weights. Be sensible and begin with a routine that suits your body. The best investment is a sensible trainer who will work with your body and help to motivate you to reach your goals. Maybe even join a gym. My grandma taught me to do the splits when I was three. Throughout the years, I regularly did them in my exercise regime and sometimes still do them in my one-woman show!

If you can do something athletic when you are young and you continue to do it as you age, you will find that you can still do it. Of course, you aren't as agile at tennis, swimming or jogging but it is still possible to be physically fit. The human body is the most sophisticated and brilliant mechanism, so don't abuse it – use it.

And for God's sake do not attempt to emulate those skinny starlets in the celeb magazines. I dread to think what those 'lollipop ladies' will look like in their fifties and sixties, after having starved and exercised themselves down to skin and bone so that they look like concentration-camp victims. These girls are asking for trouble, as it is simply not natural or attractive for the female body to look like that of an adolescent boy. Sadly too many teenagers and younger girls try dieting down to ludicrously thin proportions, which is as unhealthy and dangerous as it is for those blimps who consume Mar Bars and Alco-pops all day. I read in a magazine recently about a star who 'has an enviably boyish body'. How dreadful! What woman in her right mind wants to look like a boy?

The only men I know who think that super-skinny girls with almost-flat chests and no hips are sexy are those in the fashion world and some Hollywood types. Most straight men don't fancy them. The sad fact is that too many designer's clothes today are so shapeless and unflattering that only a stick-thin, clothes-hanger girl can make them look good, which is probably why so many women today have given up on fashionable clothes and gone for the elasticized waist, jeans and baggy T-shirt look.

And watch out, because being too thin and dieting radically in youth (or at any age) means you could be a candidate for osteoporosis in later life. But a fierce competitor for this questionable prize will also be the overweight junk-food eater, whose body has been deprived of nourishment throughout its adult life.

Balanced meals, keeping an eye on your appetite and moderate exercise means healthy bones, which are the building blocks for a long and youthful life – get the picture yet?

Let's review some tips and explore some new ones to keep you youthful, and stop you from breaking a knee, hip or anything else vital:

- Stay active. Constantly. Stretch your muscles when you wake up and throughout the day.

- Exercise, exercise, exercise – at least twenty minutes every other day of light muscle work combined with healthy walks or swims. Ideally four hours a week if you're hunched over a computer for most of the day.

- Check your eyesight every six months and make sure your prescriptions are right for you. Some opticians have a nasty habit of forcing you to wear too-strong glasses, so keep your eyes open for this! Specs can be glam but you need to chose a modern, attractive frame.

- Stay mentally alert – do crossword puzzles, play card games or board games like Scrabble, involve yourself in good conversation and debate, or simply try to answer the questions on quiz programmes before the contestants do. All this helps to keep the brain working.

- Cultivate a hobby, and I don't mean watching TV or surfing the Internet. Challenge yourself – take up gardening, painting, drawing, photography or keep scrapbooks – there are hundreds of activities that can engage and enrich you. Some of my friends have even started knitting!

- Drink at least six glasses of water a day. Tea, coffee and colas don't count. As for fizzy diet drinks, it has recently been proven that people who drink two or more of them a day actually gain *more* weight than those who drink fruit juice or cordials. Also diet drinks can dehydrate you and dehydration often leads to dizziness. Bear in mind that our bodies are about 55 to 60 per cent water, and we use up a lot of it each day, especially if you follow my advice and have a healthy physical regime.

- Women should start bone-density scans after the age of fifty, and should your doctor decide that HRT is not recommendable for you, then consider one of the various calcium supplements available today.

- Make sure your carpets and rugs are secure. So many falls happen at night when the rooms are not properly lit. A girlfriend of mine broke her leg in five places when she got up to go to the loo and fell down just two steps. Other domestic dangers are uncovered electrical flexes, too-high beds and shoes left in the middle of the floor, so be sensible – you're not twelve any more!

- Make sure your shoes fit properly. Most women's shoes today are a health hazard and should come with a warning. Much as I love my Manolos, I'm careful when I walk in them and I pick my times to wear them. Stilettos and mules are hopeless for shopping and after fifty they can be tough on the feet. Sneakers of course are safe but not always appropriate. There are other sensible and healthy shoes in the store. My first doctor in NY told me that since stilettoes became so much in vogue, his business had improved by 50 per cent due to all the falls these shoes contributed to!

- More falls occur in the shower or bath than practically anywhere else, so put in an anti-slip bath mat and be careful when clambering out of a soapy bath or shower.

- Work on your balance and flexibility. Tai Chi or yoga classes are excellent for this. Other classes, such as salsa, ballroom or tap dancing are a fabulous and fun form of exercise, with the benefit of social intercourse as well!

- Last but by no means least: POSTURE! No woman looks good slouching and with her belly sticking out. Shoulders back, stomach in and head high – 'atta girl!

wonders when my children had a cold), Salade Nicoise
(the recipe copied from my favourite Saint Tropez
restaurant, Club 55), and last but by no means least, the
world's most fabulous and fattening chocolate mousse,
again freely adapted from another wonderful restaurant in
Provence, L'Auberge de la Môle.

Apart from these culinary delights both Percy and my
children have told me I make the best tuna fish sandwiches and scrambled eggs in the world! Well, maybe
Jamie or Nigella do it better, but I'll challenge them to a
sandwich-making competition any time they want!

I am eclectic in my love of food because I like so many
things across the board, although you will rarely catch me
gnawing on a hamburger – unless it's a turkey or chicken
burger (without the bun of course). I love hot dogs and
pork sausages with fried onions, and baked beans, and all
kinds of shepherd's and cottage pie.

At the other end of the spectrum I adore caviar in a
baked potato with butter and sour cream; and Peking
duck with sliced cucumbers, spring onions, plum sauce
and pancakes, a top dish at Mr Chow in Hollywood. One
of my absolutely all-time favourites, which is a speciality
at The Wolseley restaurant, is *Soufflé Suisse* – a delectable
combination of cheese, eggs, cream and exotic flavour-
ings. A cholesterol bomb, but they serve it with lambs
lettuce or mache so that makes it a healthier option.

I adore all Mediterranean food and since I spend quite
a bit of time in the South of France that is mostly what we
eat. Practically every restaurant or bistro you go to, the

dishes are good. The French respect their food, and their mealtimes are sacrosanct. Even in the flea markets in Paris everything stops for lunch as the stallholders set out their wares on antique tables or desks and consume a hearty lunch complete with wine. I find that so civilized compared to wolfing down a sandwich with crisps and a fizzy drink. Many people condemn wine drinkers but, as with all things, moderation is the key. But then, the French understand moderation.

When we are in our villa in the South of France we consume the exquisite rosé wine with abandon. The bouquet and the taste are both delicious and invigorating, although I must confess we tend to drink it as if it were lemonade.

Much as I admire them, I blame the Americans for the super-size-me mania that has swept the world and created Orca-sized oafs. Order an iced tea at some restaurants in LA and such a colossal container arrives that you half expect a mop to be sticking out of it.

In Planet Girth, where they believe quantity often outweighs quality and where bigger is always better, nowhere does this hold truer than in southern California. In every cinema, Godzilla-sized cartons of popcorn and hot dogs with the dimensions of miniature dachshunds are wolfed voraciously, washed down with prodigious quantities of a sparkling 'beverage'. And try buying a normal-sized bar of chocolate; they are now mainly only sold in giant sizes.

America started it, but the UK has quickly followed suit. Fifty-five per cent of the American population is

considered by their government to be officially overweight, and in the UK we're rapidly catching up. (Britons
are now officially the fattest people in Europe, and fifth
only to the US, Mexico, Chile and New Zealand.) This
swelling of the *avoirdupois* has happened in a fairly short
timespan. In 1990, obesity in America affected 15 per cent
or less of the population. By 2009, it had ballooned
(excuse the pun) to a whopper-sized 30 per cent.

Obesity is soaring and the size of obese people has
doubled over the past twenty years, but I'm not surprised.
In any supermarket today the shelves are groaning with
enough goodies to cause anyone's salivary glands to shift
into top gear. For someone like me – an admitted
chocoholic – it requires supreme willpower to reach the
tills with only the basics in my basket. In any case, these
staples are either stacked too high up or too low down,
while at eye level you are assaulted by a cornucopia of
alluring food. Who was it that said a temptation resisted
is a true measure of character?

A curious spectacle in many American restaurants is
that of people taking away half their lunch or dinner
clutched in a foil container. These are the same people
who throw out containers of supermarket food when it's
one day past its sell-by date.

After appearing on an LA breakfast chat show recently,
my hunger pangs sent me scurrying into one of those
all-you-can-eat places. This is what appeared on my
plate: four fried eggs, six sausages, seven rashers of bacon,
two fried tomatoes, four mushrooms and a collapsed

sandcastle of chips. Somehow, they found room to garnish this lot with a few strawberries, and a modest sprig of limp parsley. Besides the vast array was a selection of muffins, toast, rolls and Danish pastries accompanied, with a lack of any irony, by packets of low-fat spread and low-sugar jam. I was almost put off eating but, with my hunger satisfied after only a few mouthfuls the waitress, seeing my still-full plate asked, 'Was there something wrong with it?'

In Las Vegas it was mind-boggling to observe colossal vessels of human fat battle each other like Jello warriors on the straining pavement. None of the men appeared to weigh less than 300lb and most of the women were verging on 250lb. Since Las Vegas represents a true cross-section of the US population, the nation on average must presumably consume at least 3–4,000 calories a day. The portions in most restaurants now, not just in fast-food chains, are so gargantuan that the ladies who lunch in LA often split portions between each other but still leave more on their plate. My diet tip has always been: 'The best exercise for losing weight is pushing yourself away from the table.'

A recent TV commercial made by the American fast-food chain 'Carl's Jr.' seems pretty appalling in the face of the huge obesity epidemic attacking the US and the UK. A mellow voice drones, 'What does an American man want as a snack between his big meaty breakfast. His big meaty burger for lunch, and his big meaty burger for dinner? A big meat-filled burrito, of course!' Not only is this ad hugely irresponsible in countries that are struggling with rising health-care costs due to self-perpetuated illness associated with obesity, but it's also putting the meat in all the wrong places.

But obesity is not only bad for your health but also becoming hard for day-to-day living. Some airlines are now insisting that their seriously overweight passengers must pay for two tickets, for which they will be entitled to sit on both seats. Not only is this necessary for the consumer considering the current 'seat to body-mass' ratio, but we will all benefit from this stance by having a more comfortable flight in the already stressful experience that is airline travel today.

On a recent flight from London to New York, I was installed beside a lady of – to be fair – gargantuan proportions. Parts of her *avoirdupois* oozed on to my seat as I scrunched closer to the window in a desperate effort to avoid contact with her flesh, inappropriately clad in purple Lycra bicycle shorts and a sleeveless top. When the flight attendant enquired if we wanted a hot breakfast, I said yes, but my companion growled, 'No, thank you,' vehemently recoiling as if she had been offered a bowlful of asps. I devoured my scrambled eggs, croissants and jam (not bad for early morning plane food) as my next door neighbour sniffed disdainfully while delicately sucking bottled water from a sort of baby's bottle, and occasionally glancing at my repast emitting a tiny sigh – whether of disapproval or hunger I couldn't tell.

On Food

'Are you *sure* you wouldn't like anything, ma'am?' the flight attendant enquired solicitously.

'I *never* eat breakfast,' barked my neighbour, 'Never.'

I stuffed my croissant into my mouth and stifled a smile.

At Kennedy airport, after a stop-off at the powder room en route to baggage collection, I passed a coffee and doughnut shop, and there was my fat friend, sitting at a table with a double chocolate malt and a cardboard box containing *four* doughnuts in assorted colours! These she was wolfing down as if it were her last supper.

To me, this tale sums up the tragedy (and I *do* think it's a colossal tragedy) that so many people are obese. Now that lighting a cigarette is tantamount to setting fire to Windsor Castle, overeating is acceptable, snacking almost a hobby, nay even an art form, and fast-food joints are proliferating on practically every high street. With the dreadful famine in the Sudan, it seems wrong for us to overeat.

In spite of the angry denials from the NAAFA (National Association to Advance Fat Acceptance. Yes, it exists . . .) being overweight is a serious burden to the individual, and in Britain our National Health Service is spending £2 billion each year to combat health problems scientifically proven to be directly associated with obesity, such as gastro-intestinal problems and diabetes.

Despite government warnings that we are turning into a nation of couch potatoes who have begun to put our health at risk, our waistlines keep growing. Our insane relationship with fast food and overeating is killing us, but sadly many obese people are in denial over the health risks their weight causes.

Stamped on every cigarette packet is the warning to the effect that 'Smoking Kills' – should that not be stamped on certain fat-promoting foods? The tip of the iceberg was revealed in spectacular form when a fifty-six-year-old, twenty-stone New Yorker filed suit against McDonald's, Kentucky Fried Chicken and Burger King, blaming them for his illnesses and two heart attacks. Sadly he lost, but I believe that as the crisis worsens it won't be long before thousands of other fat people follow his example.

But now the seriously overweight need not resort to going to court in order to obtain gainful rewards. All they need to do is join one of the weight-loss shows that have been spawned worldwide by *The Biggest Loser*. The popularity of these programmes and their copycats, *Celebrity Fit Club*; *Too Fat at Fifteen: Fighting Back*; *Obese*; *Jamie Oliver's Food Revolution* and *Thintervention*, all feature contestants sweating, whining, quitting and crying. The immense staying power of corporate diet regimes like WeightWatchers and the blasé acceptance of extreme measures like the gastric band and liposuction are all evidence of our obsession with food. There is even a 'Tesco Diet'! Now, honestly, I'm sure it's great but isn't it rather like a pub hosting an AA meeting?

Three in ten children are now defined as obese or overweight in Britain, where 40 per cent of our girls and

20 per cent of our boys aged between eleven and fifteen at times feel guilty about what they eat and start dieting. Many of these children mirror the comfort-eating habits of their parents – 34 per cent of girls and 21 per cent of boys are likely to eat when they are sad. Is it surprising that children are overweight when 20 per cent of them never eat fruit and when most are reared on chicken nuggets, chips, fish fingers and McDonald's, consider it normal to eat in front of the TV and, after eating, not move away from it (except perhaps to crawl over to their computer screen)?

Recently I watched the movie *Wall-E* with my grand-daughter Ava. It's a very sweet movie until the point where the humans appear in their spaceship. The plot is basically this: we humans have left the earth a wasteland of junk and are so fat that we build a huge spaceship where all we have to do is sit and have all our needs catered for while Wall-E sits on earth cleaning up our mess. Apart from Wall-E and the spaceship, I didn't see anything futuristic about it – morbid obesity *is* our reality.

It seems that food can no longer be enjoyed as the French enjoy it – it has to be consumed at a constant and frenetic pace at all hours of the day. This new fixation with 'snacking' mystifies me. During the war no one had any problems deciding whether a celery stick smeared with peanut butter was a better alternative than a granola bar – you were lucky to get a slice of Spam – but then again, the reason no one was fat during the war is that no one *could* overeat. Sugar was rationed and so was butter, meat and eggs, and as for chocolates and sweets – *fuggedaboudit*!

I ate my first banana after the war and couldn't believe it was so delicious. The selection of sweets and chocolate for kids was minimal, and if my mother gave me a Fry's chocolate bar on a Monday it had to last for a week! That's probably one of the reasons I adore chocolate so much; if it's in the house I will ferret it out like a pig going after truffles. My mother made sure we took our vitamins in the form of thick, treacly diluted orange. It appears that my generation is one of the healthiest ever *if* we don't become obese!

But mine couldn't be called a deprived childhood because it was the same for all children, none of whom were fat.

There's always a new fad diet or new fad exercise or new fad surgical intervention. No wonder we are all obsessed with food – we have it rammed down our throats twenty-four hours a day with ads that either encourage us to or prevent us from eating – we're epicurean schizophrenics.

In every major city, 'gourmet' restaurants go in and out of fashion and favour faster than skirt lengths. Last year in Hollywood, unless you'd booked well in advance, it seemed you couldn't get a reservation for lunch at a certain bistro unless you were a mogul, a model or a megastar. Now you could fire a howitzer through its window and not hit a soul. Restaurants seem to open and close faster than the swarming mouths they feed.

On Food

I sampled the newly opened Caprice in New York for the second time recently. The first time I was there it felt surreal, as if I had just stepped out of a black cab on London's Arlington Street, and when Jesus the maitre d' greeted me I expected the familiar menu to feel like a slice of home.

The black-and-white deco surroundings were equally welcoming but upon a cursory glance at the menu I felt as if I'd wandered into unfamiliar territory. 'Grilled octopus?' I exclaimed to the waiter. 'And where are the salmon fishcakes?' He looked momentarily nonplussed and called over the current maitre d' who explained that the *New York Times* had given the fishcakes a poor review and consequently they had been removed from the menu! 'That's like taking the beans out of Boston!' I said, flabbergasted.

My suspicions were confirmed when I read the review: the critic felt the food was bland. Well, of course it is! That is what an Empire was built upon. If you don't understand and admire the so-called boring British palate then don't welcome a British restaurant into your city. Some of us were *weaned* on that so-called 'nursery food', which is a wonderful alternative to the spicy, salty and excessive smorgasbord available everywhere. I thought it particularly revealing that the critic described the Caprice's golden French fries as '*salty* and delicious'. I can't bear extra salt and pepper; it is really bad for you. Everyone should realize that too much salt is a precurser to a stroke. Tsk, tsk, Mr Critic, time to check your blood pressure!

One restaurateur who has consistently got everything right over the years is Wolfgang Puck. He is the culinary messiah of Californian cuisine, and has relentlessly high standards. Spago, this charming Austrian's first restaurant, really hit the headlines in the eighties when it became the annual venue for the hottest Hollywood party of the year, Irving 'Swifty' Lazar's bash on Oscar nights, when Wolfgang's Sunset Boulevard premises would be bursting with more movie stars than you could shake a breadstick at. We'd be plied with slices of sensational pizza, topped with smoked salmon, cream cheese and caviar, followed by what I still think is the best chicken dish in the world, served with double-blanched garlic and mashed potatoes with white-truffle oil – utter heaven.

Spago Beverly Hills is still the place for those who want to experience truly gastronomic fare and see *le tout* Hollywood, although you can't smoke at the tables on the patio any more. But the food is terrific, and when a restaurant places a dozen different desserts in the middle of the table for everyone to share – well, that's my kind of place.

My other favorite Hollywood haunt is the understated but always sublime Il Piccolino. You can always tell whether the chef is truly gifted by sampling their simplest dish, and their broccoli lightly sautéed with garlic and olive oil is a must-have appetizer for me. The variety of the menu is daunting, considering that I haven't met a dish yet that isn't cooked to perfection. But infrequent travellers beware: this is very much a 'regulars' place and you have to develop a personal relationship with the owners to get a table.

'Meet you at the Ritz for tea' is surely one of the most nostalgically romantic phrases. The English have revelled in their tea for over 200 years, and although it is also the British national drink, tea at the Ritz was the hallmark of elegance for most of the twentieth century.

I remember being taken there by my grandmother as a birthday treat and my eyes were on stalks in wonderment at the sheer opulence of the place. Not only was the hotel itself magnificent, an imposing edifice in Piccadilly overlooking Green Park, but the fabulous tearoom itself was a palace of sumptuous luxury. The marble columns that framed gilded archways, the floor-to-ceiling mirrors and the glittering chandeliers made the Palm Court look almost like a movie set. The customers didn't disappoint either: beautifully dressed matrons wearing gloves and pearls sipped daintily from bone-china cups surrounded by their packages from nearby Fortnum & Mason and from Harrods; City gentlemen in grey-striped trousers and frock coats devoured the mustard-and-cress and cucumber sandwiches whilst discussing business; a few children like me sat stiffly and white-socked in the gilt chairs while staring in awe at everything as the impeccable and impassive waiters proffered a selection of goodies, each one more delicious than the last. A harpist played quietly in a corner. I scoffed down every morsel.

This was such a treat for me, as I was only used to tea at the Lyons Corner House on Oxford Street with my family two or three times a month. Lyons Corner House was a bustling, brightly lit emporium that featured teatime goodies like jam tarts, sponge cakes and biscuits, but even these paled in comparison to what was on offer at the Ritz. Sadly, it was torn down long ago and replaced by a Kentucky Fried Chicken and a McDonald's, which are apparently now the chosen teatime diet of British children. Oh dear!

As a child I'd always been fascinated by the teatime ritual, as my mother used to regale us with tales of dances at the Savoy. In the thirties *thés dansants* were all the rage for young people, and there were many rules of etiquette to be observed. It all sounded impossibly glamorous. Mummy told me that all the ladies waltzed and tangoed in floaty chiffon dresses, gently flirting with the elegantly dressed gentlemen. And her stories seemed very romantic to us, for it was at one such dance where my parents met.

The Savoy still serves fabulous afternoon teas, but the dress code has been relaxed. No one possesses a tea gown of course, although judging by fashions nowadays they could become popular again. They certainly beat crop tops and combats for style.

Only a few lucky individuals will ever experience the delights of a true epicurean English tea. Silver-tiered cake-stands hold slender finger sandwiches with traditional but light fillings such as cucumber or salmon or egg and cress, and then there are the warm scones fresh from the oven and served with clotted Devonshire cream and the finest preserves, delicate pastries and *petits fours*, cakes, tarts or *millefeuille*. Tea is served from exquisite silver pots, and poured over strainers into fine china cups.

In the movie *The Cooler*, Alec Baldwin ran a forty-year-old casino in Las Vegas that hadn't changed since it opened, complete with cocktail waitresses, corny Italian crooners and slot machines from the sixties. The mob wanted to tear it down and put up a modern multi-storeyed place but Baldwin's character rebelled, saying there were still people out there who like the old-fashioned traditional casino and that he wouldn't turn his place into a kitsch kindergarten playground where people just come and gawp at the boutiques and shopping arcades and parents in shell suits push screaming kids around in prams. 'We're a casino!' he yells. 'A real casino for real gamblers, and that will never go out of date.' Well, that summarizes how I feel when so many great restaurants are axed.

The last time I was performing in Phoenix, Arizona I stayed at the Ritz Carlton where they served a delicious tea that was just what I needed to sustain me before a performance of *Legends* with Linda Evans. The sandwiches were almost as good as I remembered, the setting was beautiful, except it was a pianist, instead of a harpist, who was terrific. Closer to home I like tea at the calm and quiet Athenaeum hotel and also at the Dorchester, where traditional tea is served in the opulent promenade and includes a glass of pink champagne; and Claridges, which is wonderfully art deco. But none of them can compare to tea at the Ritz.

The Wolseley is London's most fascinating restaurant for people-watching. It has undergone a few changes of use – originally, it was an opulent showroom for the Wolseley automobile, then it became a branch of Barclays Bank before its most recent reincarnation. The staff are extremely courteous and highly professional and the menu is delicious – it's rare for a restaurant to posses *all* these characteristics. Certainly there are many that are well staffed and which serve excellent food but the club-like atmosphere at the Wolseley is unique. Lucian Freud, arguably the world's greatest living painter is a regular there, and the place is always packed for breakfast, lunch and dinner with a large sprinkling of the rich and the famous.

The only other restaurant that has a similar 'theatrical' atmosphere is open for lunch only – the legendary Club 55 in Saint Tropez. Patrice de Colmont, the owner, runs it expertly in the high season with a turnover of at least three lunch sittings every day: the twelve o'clock group, mostly children and nannies; the two o'clock group is usually regulars and then there is the late-afternoon crowd who stumble in from their gin palaces at four o'clock where they linger until the sun and their hangovers settle.

'55' was opened in 1955, when Brigitte Bardot and Roger Vadim, while filming *And God Created Woman*, discovered the de Colmont family cooking over an open fire in a small shack on the Pampelonne Beach. The film crew made the tiny restaurant their base while filming and shortly after *Les Tout Paris* descended. Patrice, who was an infant then, grew up learning the secrets of running a fine establishment expertly from his parents. The two brothers and their sister now seem to run half of Saint Tropez – well deserved.

Patrice was recently offered €35 million by a large chain to buy the club and, although the sale would have afforded him and his family a life of ease, to say the least, he refused. When I asked him why, he said, 'And do what? Become a fat f*** with a yacht who eats at "55" every day?'

Fortunately, I don't have a yacht.

Many people mistakenly think of Saint Tropez as a resort full of beaches scattered with topless maidens (and matrons), heavy hitters and illicit sex. That certainly goes on in some of the more decadent beaches such as the Voile Rouge, where groups of rich merchants think nothing of paying €10,000 for a jeroboam of champagne, which they then liberally squirt over their squealing, scantily clad lady friends. Lunches at some of these beaches begin around 3 p.m. and rarely finish before 8 or 9 p.m., complete with floor shows and fashion parades of the flimsiest beachwear and wild, uninhibited dancing on the tables and bars to the heaviest of rap beats – it's non-stop decadence, which I have to admit can be fun.

The antithesis of '55' and the Voile Rouge is a terrific

little restaurant called Le Plage des Graniers right in the heart of Saint Tropez village and on the seashore. It's a secret only I and the French seem to know about (so far, so good). There is nothing quite as sublime as lunching whilst the sand crunches between your toes and the crystal water laps at your feet. It's simple, down-to-earth and as far from the perceived Saint Tropez as it can possibly get.

Another restaurant we frequent is the L'Auberge de la Môle in the village of La Môle, which features the most gastronomically superb five-course set menu anywhere in the area. The first and second courses consist of five distinct pâtés served in large tubs from which you may indulge to your heart's content. This is followed by frogs' legs, salade de crevettes or omelette aux cèpes. The main course is simple duck or steak, but it is the most delicious magret of duck, or my personal favourite *Tournedos Rossini*, a tender fillet topped with seared foie gras. Both are accompanied by the most succulent potato pie the world has ever known. Then of course, as in every French restaurant there's the cheese: the selection at the L'Auberge de La Môle will leave your head spinning. It will be followed by, if you can fit this in, five large tubs of dessert which, again, you can indulge in at leisure.

For anyone but the French, and the Europeans in general, the fare at L'Auberge would be a disaster of epic proportions – merely a glance at the trans-fats would cause massive heart attacks to Americans and Brits alike. But the average customer looks fit, and at ease with the delights presented to them, choosing what they want to eat and passing on what they don't. They also take their time: some tables could easily while away four to five hours over dinner. And they certainly don't go every day, or even every week. It's a special treat and the next day they just eat salad.

This is the miracle element that we seem to be missing: to enjoy and not obsess over food, which other Europeans understand in a deeply ingrained way. Europeans for the most part are fit and not fat, yet have healthy appetites. That is not to say there aren't fat people in the rest of Europe, but somehow they don't reach that morbidly obese level so common in Britain, or in America. They take pride in local fare and regional dishes, mealtimes are regular events during which one not only samples delicious food but shares it with loved ones, food is to be enjoyed and relished along with the great company that a mealtime provides and they never eat in front of the TV. This ritual is passed by example from father to son, from mother to daughter over a great many generations. I do admire the rest of Europe for having maintained a ceremony that America and Britain seem to have forgotten, confirming that an old dog can still teach the young pup a few tricks.

On Values:
Wha's Dat?

There are so many positive things that come from getting older: wisdom, tolerance and knowledge. But the older I get the more I realize how little I really know, when in the arrogance of my youth I thought I knew everything.

There are many things that the young do not possess, particularly wisdom, because how can you have wisdom if you haven't lived long enough to gain experience? I'm amazed nowadays at how so many young people think they know it all, when really all they know is who was on *Pop Idol* last week and the length of J-Lo's skirt.

*

There seems to be little sense of right and wrong with so many people today. Chastise a person in the street for dropping a food wrapper or using foul language and you'll be lucky just to get away with them screaming abuse at you. Stare for a second at a group of young people loitering on a street corner and more often than not you'll receive a thinly veiled threat along the lines of 'Whatya think you're lookin at?'

London, along with many big cities in the UK, is fraught with potential hazards. At worst, mugging, theft and verbal abuse; at best, complete indifference and a lack of basic courtesy. In some of the most violent incidents, victims appear to be chosen randomly, with often no clear indication that age, colour or creed are the motivators. Some young delinquents seem to take particular pleasure in abusing the elderly or those with special needs. I believe that we need discipline now more than ever. You have to be cruel to be kind, as my mother said as she stopped me stuffing sweets in my mouth before dinner. But discipline needs to be instilled from birth, and I don't see many parents today who know how to do this; particularly since there is so much conflicting advice. Gone are the days when you learnt how to parent your children properly from examples set by your own mum and dad.

It seems that in large towns many people possess a heart of stone in relation to other people's predicaments. I have seen young mothers struggling to board a bus, juggling a baby, a toddler, a pushchair and a bag of groceries, while other passengers just avert their eyes. I was recently told about an eighty-year-old pensioner with advanced Parkinson's disease being denied a seat on a bus by adolescent boys hunched over their mobiles, apparently oblivious of his discomfort. But the total lack of concern for the elderly and infirm in our brave new world is a sick symptom of how our society chucks them on to the slagheap of life.

If parents teach their children how to behave and what is right and what is wrong, then it is not a far stretch to realize that the media is to society what parents are to children.

The media tells us what is 'in vogue' and what is not. TV and magazines tell parents what they should buy and what they should not; what they should eat and what they should not; what they should see and what they should not.

Corporations in turn get their information from the media about which of their products will sell. Isn't it frightening that some of the bestselling products are games that promote violence and hatred – 'Grand Theft Auto', 'Manhunt' and 'Mortal Combat'? I'm not saying that the media is totally responsible for this disturbing trend, they are simply reporting the facts, and it's the facts that are disturbing.

Blogs, postings, tweets, Facebook pages, websites and even the old fashioned newspaper are devoured instantly in a world that now insists on instant, must-have, up-to-the-minute information. The freedom is almost overwhelming, but the results of that freedom are contradictory to the peaceful, tolerant world that our parents dreamed about for their children, with paedophiles, serial killers and criminals now having access to websites where they can communicate with like-minded others.

More importance must be placed on the rearing of our children both at home and at school. These two places were the birthplace of values for me. Today's schooling system seems a mystery. How can kids possibly receive a proper well-rounded education when their classes are packed to capacity? When bright kids are forced to move at the slowest pace? When their teachers are stretched to the limit and dealing with highly disruptive students? It seems there are many parents who allow their kids to run wild at home and then expect the teachers, who have their hands tied by endless regulations, to nurture them. Many teachers are bullied, assaulted, insulted and are unable to change things because of fear of the repercussions. And when some have a meltdown, unable to cope, they are summarily dismissed and ridiculed publicly. In a landmark strike recently the teachers at a Lancashire comprehensive walked out in protest at how they are treated, citing the daily anarchy in their classrooms, which they were powerless to prevent.

Decades of the liberal policies that have taken power away from teachers have eroded the educational system and in turn the fabric of our society. Some schools are even offering rewards to kids for just coming to school, never mind doing the work! There are gangs of violent pupils who care not a bit for learning or their fellow pupils, let alone their teachers. In the US, so many schools are ruled by gangs that some high schools and secondary schools have been actually forced to close down. Metal detectors and policemen on the rounds in the school hallways are no way to provide a safe and caring environment. The older pupils bully the younger ones unmercifully so their only protection, other than a knife or a gun, is to join the same gang and perpetuate the oppressive cycle. The rot in our schools isn't a momentary problem – it ruins the next generation and will continue to do so until this vicious cycle is broken.

I have many friends in business and retail who tell me that hiring a young person fresh out of school nowadays is a nightmare. Many of them don't know how to read or write properly, have no social skills and are totally unfit to become any sort of an earner.

To demonstrate how much discipline has eroded in schools today, there have been cases where children have been caught watching porn on their mobiles, had their phones confiscated and upon complaints from the parents, had the phones returned with an apology.

I also pity the children of today who are exposed to the nasty adult world of profanity, porn and poverty of thought. Kids take on board the mindless slosh that drips through TV and films today; famous footballers who brawl in bars;

slaggy 'glamour models' with silicone lips, inch long nails, clothes that show off everything and who tell the world 'their most intimate secrets' in the overwhelming mass of celebrity magazines; and foul-mouthed comedians who joke about the most disgusting things. These are the role models of today and what many kids aspire to.

When I was a child I wanted to be an actress and my parents warned me constantly that it was a tough, hard job, that I would have to study hard and start at the bottom, and that I would have to constantly face rejection. I took it all on board and have worked hard, and when the jobs didn't come along I remember what my father said: 'You get nothing in your life unless you work for it. Don't expect any handouts, don't expect to be given anything. You get what you deserve in life so you'd better work hard because there will always be someone right behind you who will be working harder.' And that's my credo, what I have tried to live by, and I think it has served me well.

But that discipline needs to be instilled from birth. How can children learn that patience is a virtue if they can get almost anything instantly? How can one teach conservation if *everything* is disposable? And how can you have respect for your elders, when so many of them are setting a bad example?

Do I sound as though I am scaremongering? I think I am merely expressing the thoughts and feelings of a majority perhaps unwilling to voice them out loud. I feel that the time for change is now, before it is too late. Let's ensure that children are properly educated; let's have proper sentencing in courts rather than some of the ridiculously lenient punishments that are currently being handed out; let's not allow the perpetrator to become the victim, as is happening again and again in our legal system. When a man was robbed recently he caught the guy and made him parade the high street with a sign that said 'I'm a thief, I stole £845'. So what happens? The thief sued his victim for 'hurt feelings'. Please! Now the victim has to pay a lawyer to fight his case. The thief, of course, gets Legal Aid.

I was brought up in an age when loitering in the streets, spitting or acting aggressively was an offence. Litter the streets in the fifties and you risked being heavily fined on the spot by a bobby on the beat. By contrast, some youths of today who are high on junk, junk food and junk music, regularly cause havoc, tipping over bins and kicking the contents of rubbish bags all over the streets. When a group doing this were recently confronted by TV presenter Nicky Campbell in South London, they countered with 'We don't give a f***. We don't come from here. This ain't our community.'

Complain about noise or feet on the seats on a train today and you risk verbal abuse at best, if not being physically attacked. Spitting is a foul and disgusting habit but it's fashionable with those glorious young role models – footballers – and it now seems to have been adopted as a tough guy stance by males everywhere. It's bad enough that many people in our parks and streets do not pick up after their dogs' business, thus leaving us to step on their mess, but now we have to have the visual assault of grown men spitting wads of gob indiscriminately in our path. This happened to me whilst I was walking in the park. I stopped to look at some flowers and inadvertently got in the way of a man who reacted by spitting on my shoe and spewing out an equally disgusting epithet.

Twenty years ago, and facing a crisis in quality of life, New York's Mayor Guiliani came up with a metaphor that explains exactly what is necessary in the face of deterioration in standards of living. If you have a house with a broken window and you don't mend it, then it won't be long until people come along and start breaking more windows in your house, figuring that if you care so little for your property, why should they? We face a similar crisis in our country, perhaps partially to do with many peoples' reluctance to take any pride in themselves and in their country (unless football is involved).

You can see a marked contrast as well between us and many other cultures. The French are full of national pride in their cities, their food, their culture; they have to be, they're French. Latin countries have a similar theory regarding personal appearance and hygiene: how they look on the outside reflects how they feel on the inside. If you take pride in your appearance, you have greater self-esteem, whereas if you don't care for yourself, why should anybody else?

Shortly after 9/11, Percy and I hung the American flag on the balcony of our Belgravia flat as a sign of solidarity with a country we both feel very close to. But whaddaya know? Within three days we had four requests to take it down, not because it was a security risk but rather because some of our neighbours found it 'offensive'. Now, the apartment is down the street from many different embassies where their national flags flutter away, so what difference does one more flag make? I thought. I was furious and of course I left the flag outside. I ruminated about the plethora of US flags that fly over all American public buildings and many, many homes, which led me to notice, when I visited Scotland and Wales over the next few months, the amount of St Andrew's Crosses and Welsh Lions hanging over stores, homes and buildings. The Americans, I knew, were patriotic, but so are the Welsh, Irish and Scots. I wish the English could be.

Last year, arriving at Mexico City's Benito Juarez airport, I studied the immigration form and wondered what I should put under race and nationality. Race was easy, Caucasian, and so I thought was nationality: English. But no, the officious official would not accept my definition. 'Is no correct,' he snapped, checking his computer, 'You can be British, Irish, Scottish or Welsh, no *English*.'

'I'm sorry? I'm not any of those, I'm *English*. That's where the language, Shakespeare and the best cab drivers in the world all come from,' I tried to joke.

He shook his head, 'Sorry, no English – you British –

write that.' He tossed another form at me and turned away, leaving me fuming and stubborn.

'OK!' I snapped and wrote British in the most illegible writing I could muster.

I admire the patriotism that the Scots, Welsh and Irish display by clinging to their nationality and their flag. But the St George's Cross seems to have a negative image. 'That's the price you pay for hundreds of years of oppression,' my husband smiles. 'When the British ruled most of the world it was considered perfectly acceptable then.'

I was incredibly impressed by how the Japanese behaved during their catastrophic earthquakes and nuclear melt-down. Since it is in their culture to be polite and courteous to one another, there was no looting, or non-civilized behaviour of any sort. The Japanese have an enormous amount of discipline drilled into them from childhood and have great respect not only for their country but also for their families and community. We could learn so much from their values and attitudes.

It was gratifying, a few years ago, to see the respect that Britain gave to the Queen Mother at her funeral. Perhaps there's hope for us yet, but the change in attitude today is quite alarming. Whilst change is inevitable, it seems to me that everything we held dear in England is being lost in favour of modernity and what the young want.

We need leaders who, like the Queen Mother,

advocate consistent benevolence and values, and we need to give them more of a platform. In our less simple and more stressful society, we need to nurture and allow older people to take their proper place in society.

Without their values, upon which this civilized society was built, new generations lose the moral compass of how to behave. In fact, without values, people forget the reason why society was important in the first place. Values are the natural progression of thinking people, as is the rebellion against them, but the pendulum has now gone full swing and I think it's about time to stop rebelling and start rebuilding our society, and make it great again.

Our values developed out of simple, obvious principles: basically don't steal, don't kill and definitely don't covet your neighbour's wife. And the preservation of these values is equally simple: care for others as if you were caring for youself.

So, once again I shall quote the Desiderata:

'Whatever your labours and aspirations,
in the noisy confusion of life keep peace with your soul.

With all its sham, drudgery and broken dreams,
it is still a beautiful world.
Be cheerful.
Strive to be happy.'